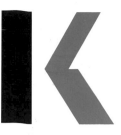

Kaplan Publishing are constantly finding new ways to make a difference to your studies and our exciting online resources really do offer something different to students looking for exam success.

This book comes with free MyKaplan online resources so that you can study anytime, anywhere. **This free online resource is not sold separately and is included in the price of the book.**

Having purchased this book, you have access to the following online study materials:

CONTENT	AAT	
	Text	Kit
Electronic version of the book	✓	✓
Progress tests with instant answers	✓	
Mock assessments online	✓	✓
Material updates	✓	✓

D1078960

How to access your online resources

Kaplan Financial students will already have a MyKaplan account and these extra resources will be available to you online. You do not need to register again, as this process was completed when you enrolled. If you are having problems accessing online materials, please ask your course administrator.

If you are not studying with Kaplan and did not purchase your book via a Kaplan website, to unlock your extra online resources please go to www.mykaplan.co.uk/addabook (even if you have set up an account and registered books previously). You will then need to enter the ISBN number (on the title page and back cover) and the unique pass key number contained in the scratch panel below to gain access. You will also be required to enter additional information during this process to set up or confirm your account details.

If you purchased through Kaplan Flexible Learning or via the Kaplan Publishing website you will automatically receive an e-mail invitation to MyKaplan. Please register your details using this email to gain access to your content. If you do not receive the e-mail or book content, please contact Kaplan Publishing.

Your Code and Information

This code can only be used once for the registration of one book online. This registration and your online content will expire when the final sittings for the examinations covered by this book have taken place. Please allow one hour from the time you submit your book details for us to process your request.

Please scratch the film to access your MyKaplan code.

Please be aware that this code is case-sensitive and you will need to include the dashes within the passcode, but not when entering the ISBN. For further technical support, please visit www.MyKaplan.co.uk

CONTENTS

Features in this exam kit

In addition to providing a wide ranging bank of real assessment style questions, we have also included in this kit:

- unit specific information and advice on assessment technique

- our recommended approach to make your revision for this particular unit as effective as possible.

You will find a wealth of other resources to help you with your studies on the Kaplan and AAT websites:

www.mykaplan.co.uk

www.aat.org.uk/

Quality and accuracy are of the utmost importance to us so if you spot an error in any of our products, please send an email to mykaplanreporting@kaplan.com with full details, or follow the link to the feedback form in MyKaplan.

Our Quality Coordinator will work with our technical team to verify the error and take action to ensure it is corrected in future editions.

INDEX TO QUESTIONS AND ANSWERS

ANSWER ENHANCEMENTS

We have added the following enhancements to the answers in this exam kit:

Key answer tips

Some answers include key answer tips to help your understanding of each question.

Tutorial note

Some answers include tutorial notes to explain some of the technical points in more detail.

ASSESSMENT TECHNIQUE

- **Do not skip any of the** material in the syllabus.

- **Read each question** *very* carefully.

- **Double-check your answer** before committing yourself to it.

- Answer **every** question – if you do not know an answer to a multiple choice question or true/false question, you don't lose anything by guessing. Think carefully before you **guess**.

- If you are answering a multiple-choice question, **eliminate first those answers that you know are wrong**. Then choose the most appropriate answer from those that are left.

- **Don't panic** if you realise you've answered a question incorrectly. Getting one question wrong will not mean the difference between passing and failing.

COMPUTER-BASED ASSESSMENTS – TIPS

- Do not attempt a CBA until you have **completed all study material** relating to it.

- On the AAT website there is a CBA demonstration. It is **ESSENTIAL** that you attempt this before your real CBA. You will become familiar with how to move around the CBA screens and the way that questions are formatted, increasing your confidence and speed in the actual assessment.

- Be sure you understand how to use the **software** before you start the assessment. If in doubt, ask the assessment centre staff to explain it to you.

- Questions are **displayed on the screen** and answers are entered using keyboard and mouse. At the end of the assessment, you are given a certificate showing the result you have achieved unless some manual marking is required for the assessment.

- In addition to the traditional multiple-choice question type, CBAs will also contain **other types of questions**, such as number entry questions, drag and drop, true/false, pick lists or drop down menus or hybrids of these.

- In some CBAs you may have to type in complete computations or written answers.

- You need to be sure you **know how to answer questions** of this type before you sit the real assessment, through practice.

KAPLAN PUBLISHING

UNIT SPECIFIC INFORMATION

THE ASSESSMENT

FORMAT OF THE ASSESSMENT

Students will be assessed by computer-based assessment.

In any one assessment, students may not be assessed on all content, or on the full depth or breadth of a piece of content. The content assessed may change over time to ensure validity of assessment, but all assessment criteria will be tested over time.

The learning outcomes for this unit are as follows:

	Learning outcome	Weighting
1	Understand and apply VAT legislation requirements	30%
2	Accurately complete VAT returns and submit them in a timely manner	40%
3	Understand the implications for the business of errors, omissions and late filing and payment	20%
4	Report VAT-related information within the organisation in accordance with regulatory and organisational requirements	10%
	Total	100%

Time allowed

1 hour 30 minutes

PASS MARK

The pass mark for all AAT CBAs is 70%.

 Always keep your eye on the clock and make sure you attempt all questions!

DETAILED SYLLABUS

The detailed syllabus and study guide written by the AAT can be found at:

www.aat.org.uk

REFERENCE MATERIAL IN YOUR ASSESSMENT

In the assessment you will be provided with comprehensive indirect tax reference material.

You can access this by clicking on the appropriate heading to the right hand side of your computer screen.

The reference material is available on the AAT website and is included at the back of the Kaplan indirect tax study text. You should have it available when you work through questions. It is important to know what is in the material and what is not!

Throughout the answers in the kit we have made reference to this material as follows:

Key answer tips

Information about this topic is included in the indirect tax reference material provided in the real assessment, so you do not need to learn it.

However you need to be familiar with its location and content – why not look at it now?

KAPLAN'S RECOMMENDED REVISION APPROACH

QUESTION PRACTICE IS THE KEY TO SUCCESS

Success in professional examinations relies upon you acquiring a firm grasp of the required knowledge at the tuition phase. In order to be able to do the questions, knowledge is essential.

However, the difference between success and failure often hinges on your assessment technique on the day and making the most of the revision phase of your studies.

The **Kaplan study text** is the starting point, designed to provide the underpinning knowledge to tackle all questions. However, in the revision phase, poring over text books is not the answer.

Kaplan pocket notes are designed to help you quickly revise a topic area; however you then need to practise questions. There is a need to progress to assessment style questions as soon as possible, and to tie your assessment technique and technical knowledge together.

The importance of question practice cannot be over-emphasised.

The recommended approach below is designed by expert tutors in the field, in conjunction with their knowledge of the chief assessor and the sample assessment.

You need to practise as many questions as possible in the time you have left.

OUR AIM

Our aim is to get you to the stage where you can attempt assessment questions confidently, to time, in a closed book environment, with no supplementary help (i.e. to simulate the real assessment experience).

Practising your assessment technique is also vitally important for you to assess your progress and identify areas of weakness that may need more attention in the final run up to the real assessment.

In order to achieve this we recognise that initially you may feel the need to practise some questions with open book help.

Good assessment technique is vital.

THE KAPLAN REVISION PLAN

STAGE 1:   ASSESS AREAS OF STRENGTH AND WEAKNESS

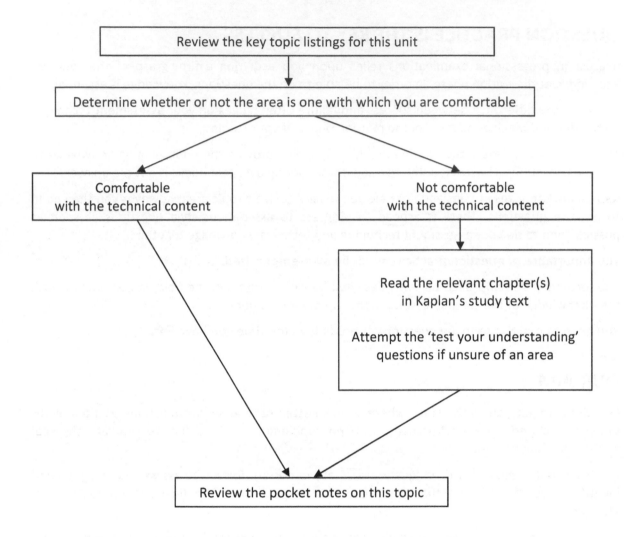

STAGE 2:   PRACTICE QUESTIONS

Follow the order of revision of topics as presented in this kit and attempt the questions in the order suggested.

Try to avoid referring to study texts and your notes and the model answer until you have completed your attempt.

Review your attempt with the model answer and assess how much of the answer you achieved.

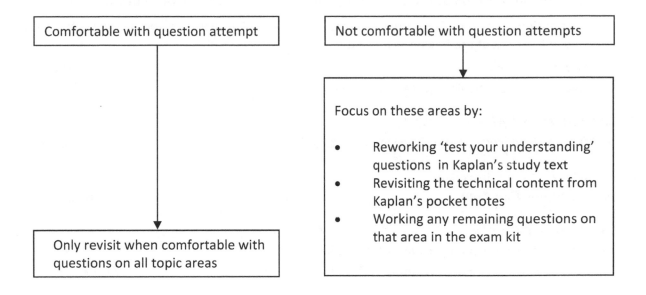

| Comfortable with question attempt | Not comfortable with question attempts |

Focus on these areas by:

- Reworking 'test your understanding' questions in Kaplan's study text
- Revisiting the technical content from Kaplan's pocket notes
- Working any remaining questions on that area in the exam kit

Only revisit when comfortable with questions on all topic areas

STAGE 3:   FINAL PRE-REAL ASSESSMENT REVISION

We recommend that you **attempt at least one full mock assessment** containing a set of previously unseen real assessment standard questions.

Attempt the mock CBA online in timed, closed book conditions to simulate the real assessment experience.

You will find a mock CBA for this unit at www.mykaplan.co.uk

TAX RATES AND ALLOWANCES

Throughout this exam kit:

1 You should assume that the reference information given below will continue to apply for the foreseeable future unless you are instructed otherwise.

2 Calculations and workings of VAT liability should be made to the nearest penny.

3 All apportionments should be made to the nearest month.

The reference information below contains key numerical information to use in this kit.

Full information is given in the indirect tax reference material available on the AAT website and is included in the back of the Kaplan study text.

Standard rate of VAT	20%
VAT fraction (standard-rated) (often simplified to 1/6)	20/120
Reduced rate of VAT	5%
VAT fraction (reduced-rated) (often simplified to 1/21)	5/105
Annual registration threshold	£85,000
De-registration threshold	£83,000
Cash accounting:	
Taxable turnover threshold (excluding VAT) to join scheme	£1,350,000
Taxable turnover threshold (excluding VAT) to leave scheme	£1,600,000
Annual accounting:	
Taxable turnover threshold (excluding VAT) to join scheme	£1,350,000
Taxable turnover threshold (excluding VAT) to leave scheme	£1,600,000
Flat rate scheme:	
Taxable turnover threshold (excluding VAT) to join scheme	£150,000
Total turnover threshold (including VAT) to leave scheme	£230,000

Section 1

PRACTICE QUESTIONS

FINDING OUT ABOUT VAT, REGISTRATION, VAT RECORDS

Key answer tips

Tasks will usually have two or three parts. Some of the questions in this section of the kit are multi-part whereas others give practice on the individual parts likely to be tested in this type of task.

Areas covered are some of the basics of VAT, particularly the registration conditions, registration and deregistration thresholds and issues concerning the record-keeping.

Learners are expected to know about relevant sources of information, the location of guidance and advice on VAT matters, the nature and powers of HMRC in respect of VAT, and how VAT is a tax on expenditure by the end consumer. Tasks may also deal with the business's relationship with HMRC, and how long to keep records.

1 HUSSEY

(a) Hussey asks you which of the following unregistered businesses is **required** to be registered for VAT. All the businesses have been trading for one year.

Select one answer.

A   A business with £86,200 of sales in the last 12 months split evenly between exempt and standard-rated supplies

B   A business with £86,200 of sales in the last 12 months split evenly between zero-rated and standard-rated supplies

C   A business with £86,200 of zero rated-sales in the last 12 months

D   A business with £86,200 of exempt sales in the last 12 months

(b) If you have a query about VAT which of the following actions should you do first?

A   Ring the HMRC helpline

B   Write to HMRC

C   Search the HMRC website

2 HUGH

Which two of the following statements are true?

(i) Hugh need not register for VAT if he has made £86,000 12 months to be £84,000.

(ii) A business has made £86,000 of sales in the last 12 months including £10,000 of sales of capital assets previously used by the business. The business is not required to register at this time.

(iii) A business which exceeds the registration threshold under the historic test on 31 July will be required to notify HMRC by 30 August and will be registered with effect from 1 September.

(iv) A business which expects to make taxable supplies of £86,000 in the next 30 days must notify HMRC by the end of the 30 day period and will be registered with effect from the end of the 30 day period.

A (i) and (ii)

B (ii) and (iii)

C (iii) and (iv)

D (i) and (iv)

3 JENKINS

Jenkins runs or part runs the following five businesses:

	Taxable supplies per year
Three sole trader businesses	£40,000 each
A business run in partnership with his wife	£100,000
A business run in partnership with his wife and brother	£90,000

How many separate VAT registrations are required to cover these businesses?

A 2

B 3

C 4

D 5

4 NASSER

(a) Nasser is thinking of registering his business for VAT voluntarily rather than waiting until his taxable turnover is over the registration threshold.

Which two of the following reasons might explain why a business would not voluntarily register for VAT?

Tick the two correct reasons.

	Would not voluntarily register
It makes their goods more expensive for other VAT-registered businesses.	
It makes their goods more expensive for businesses that are not VAT-registered.	
It helps to avoid penalties for late registration.	
It increases the business burden of administration.	

(b) What does Nasser need to demonstrate to HMRC to be able to register voluntarily? Select ONE answer.

A   That he needs to be able to recover his input tax to make his business successful

B   That he intends to make only exempt supplies

C   That he intends to make only zero-rated supplies

D   That he intends to make either zero-rated or standard-rated supplies or both

5 ISY

(a) Isy started a business on 1 December. Her monthly sales are £12,000 split equally between standard-rated, zero-rated and exempt supplies.

On what date will she exceed the compulsory VAT registration threshold?

A   Never

B   30 June

C   31 October

D   30 November

(b) Jo runs a small sole trader business which is registered for VAT. Her business is taken over as a going concern by another sole trader Dorrit. Dorrit runs a similar business which is currently not registered for VAT. The combined turnover of the new business will be £190,000.

Can the VAT registration of Jo's business be transferred across to the new combined business?   YES/NO

6 VOLUNTARY DEREGISTRATION

Can the following VAT-registered traders deregister their business **voluntarily**?

Tick one box on EACH line.

	Yes	No
A business which is ceasing to trade.		
A continuing business which expects to make supplies of £83,000 in the next year of which one quarter will be exempt supplies.		
A business which expects to make taxable supplies of £84,000 in the next 12 months.		
A continuing business which has been making taxable supplies of £87,000 per year but which has now switched to making wholly exempt supplies of the same amount.		

7 DOOKU

Dooku is considering the purchase of one of the following unregistered businesses and wants to know if he should register them for VAT immediately or monitor turnover and register later.

Tick one box on EACH line

	Register now	Monitor and register later
A business with £50,000 of taxable turnover in the last 11 months but which expects taxable turnover of £87,000 in the next 30 days.		
A business with taxable turnover of £5,000 per month for last 12 months.		
A business with taxable turnover of £7,500 per month for the last 12 months.		
A business with turnover of standard-rated supplies of £4,000 per month for the last year but which expects turnover of £50,000 in the next 30 days.		

8 CERTIFICATE OF REGISTRATION

(a) Why is a VAT certificate of registration important?

Choose ONE answer.

A   It is proof that the business has started to trade

B   It is proof that the business is entitled to charge output VAT

C   It is proof of the trader's VAT registration number

(b)   Which of the following are powers of HMRC in respect of VAT?

Tick one box on each line.

	Is a power	Is not a power
Charging penalties for breaches of VAT rules		
Completing VAT returns		
Inspecting premises		
Providing suitable books for VAT record keeping		
Changing the rate of VAT		

9   REMONA

Which one of the following statements is correct?

Select ONE answer.

A   Remona should have registered on 1 September but did not register. Since that time she has invoiced sales of standard-rated goods totalling £15,000. She will be liable for output VAT of £3,000.

B   The taxable turnover for the historic registration test can be measured at any time, not just the end of the month.

C   When a trader fails to register on time they can be charged a penalty of up to 100% of the tax due.

D   All registered traders submit VAT returns quarterly.

10   RHYS

Rhys asks you which of the following statements is INCORRECT.

Select ONE answer.

A   Only registered businesses can charge VAT to customers.

B   VAT is a charge which is ultimately suffered by the end consumer.

C   A business making £60,000 of exempt supplies and £20,000 of zero-rated supplies cannot register for VAT.

D   Many VAT queries can be answered by referring to the HMRC website.

11   TROI

Troi has a business which makes standard-rated and zero-rated supplies but is not yet registered for VAT.

She has given you the following details about her sales.

	Monthly turnover	
	Standard-rated	Zero-rated
	£	£
Year ended 31 December 20X5	2,000	4,000
January 20X6	2,500	3,100
February 20X6	6,500	4,600
March 20X6	8,900	6,200
April 20X6 and thereafter	8,700	5,900

At the end of which month does Troi exceed the registration threshold?

A   February 20X6

B   March 20X6

C   April 20X6

D   December 20X6

12   BARCLAY

Barclay asks you why it is important to keep up-to-date with VAT rules. Which one of the following is NOT a good reason to keep up-to-date?

Select ONE answer.

A   It helps you to ensure that the business avoids VAT penalties.

B   It is important for the ethical principle of professional competence to keep up-to-date.

C   It helps you to know when the business should register for VAT.

D   It helps you to know how the business may evade VAT.

13   LO

Lo has asked you to advise which of the following statements about records required for VAT purposes are true and which false.

Tick one box on EACH line.

	True	False
Businesses must keep records of all taxable and exempt supplies made in the course of business.		
Taxpayers need permission from HMRC before they start keeping records electronically.		
All businesses must keep a VAT account.		
The balance on the VAT account represents the VAT payable to HMRC or repayable by HMRC.		
Sending or receiving invoices by electronic means is permitted but paper copies must also be kept.		
Records should normally be kept for at least 3 years before being destroyed.		
Failure to keep records can lead to a penalty.		

VAT INVOICES, TAX POINT, MAKING EXEMPT SUPPLIES

Key answer tips

Tasks will usually have two or three parts. Some of the questions in this section of the kit are multi-part whereas others give practice on the individual parts likely to be tested in this area.

Candidates are expected to know about VAT invoices and their content, the use of simplified invoices, the tax point for each supply and the implications of exempt supplies.

Other areas include the time limits for issuing invoices, the nature of input and output tax, pro-forma invoices, the basics of partial exemption and the implications for input tax reclaim of making exempt and zero-rated supplies.

14 CAIN

(a) Cain runs a VAT-registered business. On 4 May he receives an order for goods from a customer. On 15 May the goods are delivered and on 20 May Cain issues a tax invoice. The customer pays on 28 June.

What is the tax point date?

A   4 May

B   15 May

C   20 May

D   28 June

(b) Clarence is a VAT-registered trader. He raises a pro-forma invoice in advance of making a supply. The pro-forma invoice is dated 17 August. Payment is received on 20 August and the goods are delivered on 24 August. A VAT invoice is sent to the customer on 31 August.

What is the tax point date?

A   17 August

B   20 August

C   24 August

D   31 August

(c) Drogba is a VAT-registered trader. He receives an order for standard-rated goods on 1 February, delivers the goods to the customer on 7 February, raises and sends a tax invoice on 28 February and receives payment on 19 March.

What is the tax point date?

A   1 February

B   7 February

C   28 February

D   19 March

15 RATTAN

(a) Rattan is a VAT-registered trader. She receives an order for standard-rated goods on 11 April, delivers the goods to the customer on 19 April, raises and sends an invoice on 8 May and receives payment on 24 May.

What is the tax point date?

A   11 April

B   19 April

C   8 May

D   24 May

(b) Sisal runs a VAT-registered business. He received an order from a customer on 13 October. He delivered the goods to the customer on 24 October and issued a tax invoice on 29 October. The customer paid for the goods on 6 December.

What is the tax point date?

A   13 October

B   24 October

C   29 October

D   6 December

(c) Reed is a VAT-registered trader. He receives a deposit from a customer on 16 July. The goods are delivered to the customer on 24 July and a VAT invoice is sent to the customer on 4 August. The customer settles the balance of the invoice on 2 September.

What is the tax point date in respect of the deposit?

A   16 July

B   24 July

C   4 August

D   2 September

16 ROGER

Roger is registered for VAT and all of his supplies are standard-rated. He requires a 20% deposit from his customers within 10 days of receiving an order.

What are the tax points for the deposit and the balance in each of the following?

Complete the table with the appropriate dates.

Deposit paid	Goods delivered	Invoice raised	Balance paid	Tax point for deposit	Tax point for balance
10 March	12 March	30 March	18 March		
21 February	7 March	10 March	1 April		
13 May	26 May	11 June	7 July		

17 BOLD

(a) Bold is a VAT-registered trader who makes a mixture of standard-rated and zero-rated supplies. He makes a wholly zero-rated supply to Zed Ltd delivering the goods on 20 July and issuing an invoice on 25 July. He receives payment on 31 July.

Which of the following statements are true?

Tick one box for each line.

	True	False
The tax point date is 20 July.		
The tax point date is 25 July.		
An invoice for a wholly zero-rated supply is not a tax invoice.		
Input tax recovery in respect of zero-rated supplies is restricted.		

(b) This is a shop invoice for a cash purchase.

	Wealdstone Supplies, 14, Western Rd, Cleethorpes VAT registration number: 123 4567 89 Date: 16 October 20X2	
Quantity		£
1	Dishwasher	420.00
	Total due	420.00
	VAT 20% included	Cash paid

Is this a valid VAT invoice? Select one of the options below.

A   Yes it is a valid VAT invoice

B   Yes it is a valid simplified VAT invoice

C   Neither of the above

18 RANKIN

Rankin is a registered trader and sells only standard-rated goods. His normal terms of trade insist on a 15% deposit as part payment for all sales made. The deposit has to be paid before goods are delivered.

What are the tax points for the deposit and the balance in each of the following?

Complete the table with the appropriate dates.

Deposit paid	Goods delivered	Invoice raised	Balance paid	Tax point for deposit	Tax point for balance
28 June	14 July	17 July	5 August		
19 October	31 October	16 November	12 December		
2 December	4 December	22 December	10 December		

19   MARGARET

(a)   Margaret is a VAT-registered trader. She receives a supplier credit note and processes it in her quarter ended 30 September.

What will be the effect on VAT?

Choose one answer.

A   Output tax will increase

B   Output tax will decrease

C   Input tax will increase

D   Input tax will decrease

(b)   A UK business issues a sales invoice for taxable supplies to a VAT-registered EU customer.

What is the effect on VAT for the UK business?

Choose one answer.

A   Output tax will increase

B   Output tax will stay the same

C   Input tax will decrease

D   Output tax will decrease

20   MARGOT

Margot is having trouble dealing with credit notes and debit notes. She makes the following statements and wants you to tell her which are true and which false.

Tick one box on EACH line.

	True	False
The receipt of a credit note from a supplier will reduce her output tax.		
The issue of a debit note to a supplier will reduce her input tax.		
The issue of a credit note to a customer will reduce her output tax.		
The receipt of a debit note from a customer will reduce her output tax.		

21   JONSSON

(a)   Jonsson does not make sales to the public.

Which of the following does Jonsson NOT have to include on his sales invoices to other UK businesses?

A   Name and address of the supplier

B   Name and address of the customer

C   VAT registration number of the customer

D   The tax-exclusive value of the invoice

(b)   Which of the following does Jackson, a retailer, NOT have to include on his simplified invoices?

Select one answer.

A   Time of supply

B   Description of each item supplied

C   Rate of VAT applicable to the supply

D   Invoice number

22   AHMED

Ahmed is just starting in business and wants his invoices to comply with VAT rules. He gives you the following list of some of the things he is proposing to include.

Which items are required for a full VAT invoice?

Tick one box for each line.

	Required	Not required
Time of supply		
Customer order number		
Description of the type of supply		
Rate of VAT applicable		
General terms of trade		
Total amount payable excluding VAT		
Total amount of VAT payable		
Acceptable methods of payment		

23   NERISSA

Nerissa is a VAT-registered trader. She has decided to start issuing pro-forma invoices.

Mark each one of the following statements about pro-forma invoices as true or false.

	True	False
Pro-forma invoices must show the VAT registration number of the supplier.		
Pro-forma invoices are a way of obtaining payment before goods are despatched.		
The purchaser can use a pro-forma invoice to recover input VAT.		

24   CHEN

(a)   Chen is a VAT-registered trader. He issues a sales credit note to a customer.

What will be the effect on VAT?

Choose one answer.

A   Input tax will increase

B   Input tax will decrease

C   Output tax will increase

D   Output tax will decrease

(b)   Wing is a VAT-registered trader. He receives a supplier credit note.

What effect will this have on the amount of VAT due to HMRC?

Choose one answer.

A   The amount payable will decrease

B   The amount payable will increase

25   EFFIE

(a)   Effie wishes to issue simplified (less detailed) invoices.

What is the invoice limit above which less detailed invoices cannot be issued?

A   £50

B   £100

C   £200

D   £250

(b)   Alice, who is a retailer, issues detailed and simplified invoices. She asks you which invoice copies she should keep.

Select one option.

A   Simplified invoices only

B   Detailed invoices only

C   Both

D   Neither

26   PUCK

Puck's business is VAT-registered and supplies goods that are a mix of standard-rated and exempt.

Which of the following statements is true?

Choose one answer.

A   None of the input VAT can be reclaimed

B   Input VAT on items used to make exempt supplies can never be recovered

C   Some of the input VAT can be reclaimed, in proportion to the different types of supply

D   All of the input VAT can always be reclaimed

27 JERRY

Jerry is confused about the difference between making zero-rated and exempt supplies. He makes the following statements and wants you to tell him which are true and which false.

Tick one box on EACH line.

	True	False
Traders who make only exempt supplies cannot register for VAT.		
Traders who only make zero-rated supplies have to register for VAT.		
Zero-rated supplies made by a registered trader are not classed as taxable supplies.		
Traders making only exempt supplies cannot recover input tax.		
VAT-registered traders making a mix of zero-rated and exempt supplies cannot recover any input tax.		

28 SALLY

Sally wants to know if she can issue simplified invoices for the following supplies.

Tick one box on EACH line. All figures are VAT-exclusive.

	Can be issued	Cannot be issued
Standard-rated supplies of £210		
Standard-rated supplies of £170 plus zero-rated supplies of £40		
Standard-rated supplies of £170 plus exempt supplies of £40		

29 JORDANNE

Jordanne sells goods on a sale or return basis and specifies that the goods must be accepted or returned within four months of delivery.

Goods are delivered on a sale or return basis to a customer on 6 May with a deadline for acceptance or return by 6 September.

The customer does not formally notify Jordanne that they wish to keep the goods but sends a payment for them on 12 August.

Jordanne issues an invoice to the customer on 31 August.

What is the tax point date in respect of these goods?

A 6 May

B 12 August

C 31 August

D 6 September

30   SCOTTY

Scotty sells goods on a sale or return basis. Customers have to pay a deposit of 10% of the cost of the goods which is refunded if the goods are returned within six months.

A customer pays a 10% deposit on 2 March and receives the goods on a sale or return basis on 4 March.

On 10 June they notify Scotty that they wish to keep the goods.

Scotty issues an invoice dated 21 June and receives the remaining 90% of the cost on 11 July.

Which one of the following statements is true?

A   There are two tax points: one on 2 March for 10% of the cost, and one on 10 June for the remaining 90%.

B   There are two tax points: one on 2 March for 10% of the cost, and one on 21 June for the remaining 90%.

C   There is one tax point on 10 June.

D   There is one tax point on 21 June.

31   KIM

Kim provides accountancy services.

On 15 November he commences preparing financial statements for a client and finishes this work on 3 December.

He issues an invoice to the client on 18 December and receives payment on 29 December.

What is the tax point date in respect of these services?

A   15 November

B   3 December

C   18 December

D   29 December

32   BYRON

Byron runs a business leasing plant and machinery to customers for periods of 2 to 4 years. At the end of the lease period the plant and machinery is returned to Byron.

Customers pay a regular monthly amount by direct debit on the 20th of each month.

Which of the following statements are true and which false?

Tick one box on each line.

	True	False
If Byron invoices his customers on the last day of each month then that day will be the tax point.		
If Byron invoices his customers on the last day of each month then the tax point will be the 20th of each month.		
Byron can invoice his customers annually in advance, setting out the schedule of payments for the year. If he does this his customers will be able to recover input tax for the year on receipt of that invoice, as the invoice date will be the tax point.		
Byron can invoice his customers annually in advance, setting out the schedule of payments for the year. If he does this there will be twelve separate monthly tax points.		

33   DONNE

Donne runs a business in which 70% of her sales are taxable supplies and 30% exempt supplies.

She divides her input tax into three parts: that relating to taxable supplies, that relating to exempt supplies, and that relating to overheads.

Select which of the following statements is true.

A   Only the input tax relating to taxable supplies can be recovered

B   All of the input tax relating to taxable supplies can be recovered. It is also possible to recover 70% of the input tax relating to the exempt supplies and overheads provided this amount does not exceed a de minimis figure

C   Recoverable input tax can only ever comprise that relating to taxable supplies plus 70% of that relating to overheads

D   It is possible to recover all the input tax provided that the input tax relating to exempt supplies plus 30% of the input tax relating to overheads does not exceed the de minimis figure

VAT SCHEMES, DUE DATES, IRRECOVERABLE DEBT RELIEF

Key answer tips

Tasks will usually have two or three parts. Some of the questions in this section of the kit are multi-part whereas others give practice on the individual parts likely to be tested in this type of task.

In these tasks the candidates' knowledge of the three main accounting schemes available to businesses is tested – the annual accounting, cash accounting and the fixed rate scheme.

In addition there are sub-tasks covering the due dates for submission of returns and payment, the basics of claiming back input tax, the statutory requirement for online filing and the availability of irrecoverable debt (bad debt) relief.

34 WYE LTD

Wye Ltd has not joined any of the special accounting schemes. Its quarterly return period ends on 31 July.

By what date should its VAT return be submitted?

Select one answer.

A   31 August

B   6 September

C   7 September

D   None of the above

35 RAVI

Ravi has asked you to advise him whether the following statements about businesses that have not joined any special accounting schemes are true or false.

Tick one box for EACH line.

	True	False
VAT is normally payable at the same time that the return is due.		
Paying VAT by direct debit gives the business an extra 5 bank working days from the normal payment date before payment is taken from the account.		
New businesses have a choice about whether they submit returns electronically or on paper.		
Quarterly VAT returns are all made up to 30 April, 31 July, 31 October and 31 January.		

36 ANNUAL ACCOUNTING

(a)   What is the turnover threshold for eligibility to join the annual accounting scheme? Select ONE answer.

A   Estimated turnover in the next 12 months is not more than £150,000

B   Estimated turnover in the next 12 months is not more than £230,000

C   Estimated turnover in the next 12 months is not more than £1,350,000

D   Estimated turnover in the next 12 months is not more than £1,600,000

(b)   With the annual accounting scheme, one VAT return is made each year.

How many months after the end of the accounting period end is the return due?

Choose one answer.

A   1 month

B   2 months

C   3 months

(c)   Exe Ltd is a company that sells children's clothing. This is a zero-rated activity.

Is Exe Ltd likely to benefit from joining the annual accounting scheme?

A   Yes

B   No

(d)   Queue Ltd is a VAT-registered business whose turnover of taxable supplies has been declining for several years.

Is Queue likely to benefit from joining the annual accounting scheme?

A   Yes

B   No

37   ZED LTD

Zed Ltd is a company that uses the annual accounting scheme for VAT with monthly payments. Its VAT liability for the previous accounting period was £72,900.

What is its monthly payment on account for the current year?

A   12 monthly payments of £6,075

B   12 monthly payments of £5,468

C   9 monthly payments of £7,290

D   9 monthly payments of £8,100

38   TARAN

Taran runs a VAT-registered business and needs more information about the annual accounting scheme.

Which of the following statements are true and which false?

Tick one box for EACH line.

	True	False
Taxpayers must be up-to-date with their VAT payments before they are allowed to join the scheme.		
Monthly payments on account are 10% of the previous year's VAT liability.		
Monthly payments can be made using any method convenient to the taxpayer.		
Monthly payments are made 7 days after the end of the month.		
Monthly payments are made at the end of months 2 to 10 in the accounting period.		
The scheme allows businesses to budget for their VAT payments more easily.		

39 ARTHUR

Which of the following statements on the subject of cash accounting are true?

Select TWO answers.

A   Input VAT is reclaimed by reference to the date the supplier is paid

B   Traders can join the scheme provided their annual taxable turnover does not exceed £1,600,000

C   VAT invoices do not need to be sent to customers

D   Arthur is a VAT-registered trader whose annual turnover excluding VAT is £400,000. He has never had any convictions for VAT offences. He is eligible to join the cash accounting scheme

40 LAREDO

Laredo is a VAT-registered trader who has adopted the cash accounting scheme. He receives an order from a customer on 13 March and despatches the goods on 20 March. He invoices the customer on 24 March and receives payment on 2 May.

What is the tax point date?

A   13 March

B   20 March

C   24 March

D   2 May

41 CASH ACCOUNTING

Would the following VAT-registered businesses benefit from joining the cash accounting scheme?

Tick one box on EACH line.

	Will benefit	Will not benefit
A manufacturing business that sells all its output on credit to other businesses. Debtors take on average 45 days to pay. The business aims to pay creditors within 30 days of receiving purchase invoices.		
A clothes shop based in a town centre which sells standard-rated supplies to members of the public for cash.		
A wholesaler who sells to other businesses on 40 days credit. In the last 12 months the business has suffered a steep rise in irrecoverable (bad) debts.		
A business making solely zero-rated supplies to other businesses.		

42   FLAT RATE SCHEME

Would the following VAT-registered businesses benefit from joining the flat rate scheme?

	Will benefit	Will not benefit
A business making solely zero-rated supplies to other businesses.		
A business with a lower than average (for their trade sector) level of input tax.		
A business with a higher proportion of standard-rated supplies than other businesses in the same trade sector.		

43   RAY

Ray makes the following statements about the flat rate scheme.

Which of the statements are true and which false?

Tick one box on EACH line.

	True	False
A business can join the flat rate scheme provided its taxable turnover for the next 12 months is expected to be less than £230,000.		
VAT due to HMRC is calculated as a fixed percentage of VAT-inclusive taxable turnover.		
VAT invoices must still be issued.		
A business can be in both the flat rate scheme and the annual accounting scheme at the same time.		
The scheme cuts down on the time spent on VAT administration.		
Businesses cannot pay less VAT under the flat rate scheme than the normal method of accounting for VAT.		

44   DERNBACH

In the last quarter, Dernbach has made sales as follows:

	£
Standard-rated sales (including VAT)	22,470
Zero-rated sales	4,500
Exempt sales	1,110

The normal flat rate percentage for her type of business is 8%. The business is a limited cost business.

What is her VAT payable for the quarter?

A   £3,707.55

B   £2,246.40

C   £4,633.20

D   £4,015.27

45   SELDON

Seldon wishes to claim irrecoverable (bad) debt relief on a sales invoice to Holmes Ltd with VAT of £145.

Which of the following are NOT requirements for Seldon to be able to claim VAT irrecoverable (bad) debt relief?

Select two answers.

A   The debt must have been written off in the accounting records for at least three months before the claim is made

B   Seldon has already paid over the output tax of £145 to HMRC

C   Holmes Ltd has been placed into liquidation

D   Six months have passed since the invoice was due for payment

DETAILED VAT RULES, SURCHARGES, PENALTIES AND CORRECTIONS

Key answer tips

Tasks will usually have two or three parts. Some of the questions in this section of the kit are multi part whereas others give practice on the individual parts likely to be tested in this type of task.

These tasks cover some of the detailed VAT rules and the issues of surcharges, penalties and correction of errors, changes in legislation, imports and exports including transactions within the EU, rules on entertainment, vehicles, deposits and advance payments, use of fuel scale charges and the rules on notification of errors.

46   LUIGI

Luigi's business is VAT-registered and supplies goods that are a mix of standard-rated and zero-rated.

Which of the following statements is true?

Choose one answer.

A   None of the input VAT can be reclaimed

B   All of the input VAT can be reclaimed provided certain conditions are met

C   Some of the input VAT can be reclaimed, in proportion to the different types of supply

D   All of the input VAT can be reclaimed

47   FORTE

Forte runs a manufacturing business which makes only standard-rated supplies. During March the business incurs expenditure of £890 on staff entertaining, £456 on UK customer entertaining and £9,150 on a second hand van. All figures include VAT at 20%.

What input VAT can be claimed in respect of these three items?

A   £1,749.33

B   £1,673.33

C   £1,601.00

D   £2,008.00

48   VINCENZO

Vincenzo's business is VAT-registered. During June it makes the following cash payments.

Select Yes or No in the right hand box to show whether the input VAT can be reclaimed on the next VAT return.

Description	Net £	VAT £	Gross £	Reclaim input VAT?
Repairs to machinery	1,900.00	380.00	2,280.00	Yes/No
Delivery van	10,000.00	2,000.00	12,000.00	Yes/No
UK customer entertaining	640.00	128.00	768.00	Yes/No
Overseas customer entertaining	310.00	62.00	372.00	Yes/No
Car (pool car with no private use)	8,400.00	1,680.00	10,080.00	Yes/No

49   HOOCH LTD

Hooch Ltd is a VAT-registered business. The sales manager is provided with a company car and fuel which he uses for both business and private purposes.

The car has CO_2 emissions of 155 g/km for which the quarterly fuel scale charge is £295. Petrol paid for by the company for the car in the last quarter amounted to £822.50. Both figures are VAT-inclusive.

What is the net effect of these on Hooch Ltd's VAT for the quarter?

A   VAT payable increases by £105.50

B   VAT payable increases by £87.92

C   VAT payable decreases by £87.92

D   VAT payable decreases by £186.24

50   RAFA AND CO

Rafa and Co wish to avoid paying VAT fuel scale charges in respect of employees' motor expenses.

Which of the following mean they still have to pay a VAT scale charge?

A   The business will only reclaim VAT on fuel used for business mileage and will keep detailed records of business and private mileage driven by employees

B   The business will not reclaim any VAT on fuel

C   The business will only allow employees to claim expenses for fuel for business mileage and will reclaim all input VAT on fuel

D   The business will allow employees to claim 50% of their total fuel costs in their expense claims. The business will then reclaim the input VAT on these 50% costs

51   FINIAN

Finian sells a number of capital assets over the year.

Complete the table to show the amount of output VAT that must be charged on the sale of each item.

Item	Input tax recovered	Sale proceeds (excluding VAT)	Output VAT
		£	£.pp
Computer	Yes	400	
Car	Yes	7,500	
Van	Yes	6,100	
Car	No	8,400	

52   ALBERT

Albert is a registered trader who makes only standard-rated supplies.

In his latest VAT quarter he has spent £780 on a party for all his staff. Each member of staff brought a guest and exactly half the cost of the party was for these guests. Albert also spent £545 on UK customer entertaining and £10,700 on a second hand lorry.

All figures include VAT.

How much input tax can Albert claim on these costs?

A   £2,004.16

B   £1,913.33

C   £1,848.33

D   £2,218.00

53 VICTORIA LTD

Victoria Ltd provides a car for an employee who uses the car for both business and private purposes. All running expenses of the car are paid for by the company including fuel.

Which one of the following statements is true?

A   The company can include all the VAT on running costs in input tax but must then reduce their input tax claim by an amount determined by a scale charge

B   The company cannot recover any VAT on the running costs

C   There is no effect on VAT

D   The company can recover all the VAT on running costs but must add an amount to output tax determined by a scale charge

54 WELLES

Welles is a VAT-registered trader who has not adopted any of the special VAT accounting schemes.

Which one of the following statements about recovery of input tax on the purchase of goods is not true?

A   Welles needs to have paid for the goods

B   A VAT invoice is usually needed to support the claim

C   The goods or services must be for business use

D   Input tax cannot be recovered on goods used for UK customer entertaining

55 MELINDA

Melinda is a VAT-registered trader who has suffered input tax on the following purchases over the last quarter.

Can Melinda recover input VAT on these items?

Tick one box on each line.

	Recover	Cannot recover
Purchases for resale		
New laptop computer for Melinda's daughter		
New desk for the office (Melinda has lost the VAT receipt)		
Motorcycle for business deliveries		

56 VAT PENALTIES

Which of the statements are true and which false?

Tick one box on EACH line.

	True	False
Tax avoidance is a criminal offence and means using illegal means to reduce tax liability.		
A penalty can be charged if a trader fails to register at the correct time.		
A registered trader who makes an error on a return leading to underpayment of tax will always be charged a penalty.		
If a registered trader does not submit a VAT return then HMRC can issue an assessment to collect VAT due.		
A penalty can be charged if a trader fails to notify a significant change in their types of supply to HMRC within 30 days.		

57 VAT ERRORS

(a) For each of the following businesses, indicate with a tick whether the non-deliberate error can be corrected on the next VAT return or whether separate disclosure is required.

	Net error £	Turnover £	Include in next return	Separate disclosure
1	23,768	2,000,000		
2	7,150	85,400		
3	35,980	4,567,090		
4	61,600	10,000,000		

(b) A business finds the following non-deliberate errors made in the previous quarter.

(i) VAT on a sales credit note has been recorded as £18 instead of £81.

(ii) VAT of £21.14 on a supplier invoice has been entered twice.

What is the net error?

£

Will the error increase or reduce the VAT due on the next return?

Increase/reduce

58 DEFAULT SURCHARGE

(a) Which of the following statements about the default surcharge are correct?

Tick one box on each line.

	True	False
A default only occurs when a business pays its VAT late.		
A surcharge liability notice lasts for 6 months from the end of the period of default.		
Once a trader has received a surcharge liability notice, he must keep all his returns and payments up-to-date for the period of the surcharge notice, otherwise it will be extended.		

(b) If Exe Ltd submits its VAT return late for the first time, what is the effect?

Select one answer.

A   A surcharge of 5% of VAT due is charged

B   A surcharge liability notice is issued

C   Both of the above

D   Neither of the above

59 KEIKO LTD

Keiko Ltd is a business that uses the cash accounting scheme. All sales and purchases are standard-rated.

You are given the following information for the quarter ended 31 May 20X5:

	£
Sales invoices issued for credit sales	42,568
Purchase invoices received from suppliers	29,580
Cash sales receipts	780
Receipts from customers	39,745
Cash paid to suppliers	27,890
Petty cash – purchases of standard-rated items	175

Calculate the VAT due for the quarter to 31 May 20X5.

£

60 NOTICE

(a) A business has received a surcharge liability notice from HMRC.

Complete the following statements by choosing one option in each case.

The notice would only have been issued if the business (had missed the due date for submitting its VAT return/ had failed to register for VAT at the correct time).

The notice (imposes an immediate penalty/puts the business in a surcharge period for 12 months/ requires the business to pay over all outstanding output tax immediately).

(b) A surcharge liability notice will not be issued if the trader has a reasonable excuse for submitting their return or paying their VAT late.

Which of the following is not an example of a reasonable excuse?

A   the employee who prepares the return is on sick leave and no-one else knows how to complete the return

B   a major client has gone into liquidation and caused you to have an unexpected cash crisis

C   your customers have been late in paying your invoices recently leaving you with a lack of funds to pay

D   there was a fire in the office which destroyed the accounting records from which the return is compiled

61 STANDARD PENALTIES

Which of the following offences may result in a standard penalty?

(i)   Failure to register for VAT when it is compulsory to do so

(ii)   Submission of a late return

(iii) Late payment of VAT

(iv) Careless or deliberate error on a VAT return

A   (i) and (ii)

B   (ii) and (iii)

C   (iii) and (iv)

D   (i) and (iv)

62 ERRORS AND OMISSIONS

For each of the following errors or omissions, insert in the table below the letter that explains the appropriate action from the list below.

Appropriate actions:

A   Trader must correct the error.

B   HMRC can issue an assessment to collect tax due.

C   HMRC can issue assessment to collect tax due and charge a penalty.

D   Trader must correct the error and HMRC can charge a penalty.

Error/omissions	Action
Failing to register	
Failure to submit a return	
Making a careless or deliberate error	
Making a non-careless error	

63   PLACE OF SUPPLY

Evans runs a business situated in the UK. He is about to start selling goods and services to overseas customers within the EU. Some of the customers are registered for VAT and some are not.

Complete the table showing the place of supply of the goods and services to overseas customers within the EU.

	Place of supply in UK	Place of supply in overseas country
Goods sold to unregistered customers		
Goods sold to VAT registered customers		
Services supplied to unregistered customers		
Services supplied to VAT registered customers		

VAT CALCULATIONS AND RECONCILIATIONS

Key answer tips

Tasks will usually have two or three parts. The questions in this section of the kit give practice on the individual parts likely to be tested in this type of task.

These tasks cover some VAT calculation routines, plus reconciliation issues.

Topics include calculating tax on both gross and net supplies, what happens to the calculation of VAT when a discount is offered, and checking VAT returns to the VAT account which a VAT-registered business must keep.

64   MURRAY LTD

At 31.3.X0, the VAT control account of Murray Ltd showed a balance due to HMRC of £4,937.50. The VAT return for the quarter to 31.3.X0 showed VAT due of £2,452.10.

Which of the following explains the difference?

Choose one answer.

A   A VAT payment to HMRC of £2,485.40 has been included twice in the VAT control account

B   Output VAT of £2,485.40 has been included twice in the VAT control account

65 DARCY

At the end of the quarter, Darcy's VAT control account shows a balance due to HMRC of £3,946.82. The calculations for the VAT return show a balance due to HMRC of £3,814.32.

Which of the following explains the difference?

Choose one answer.

A   A bad debt (irrecoverable debt) of £795.00 (VAT-inclusive) which had previously been written off has now been recovered. The adjustment for this has been made in the VAT return calculations but not in the control account.

B   A credit note received on the last day of the quarter from a supplier, amounting to £662.50 excluding VAT, has been included in the VAT control account but not in the VAT return calculations.

66 BINGLEY

At the end of the quarter, Bingley's VAT control account shows a balance of VAT recoverable from HMRC of £2,947.64.

After reviewing the records, the following items have been found which may affect the balance of VAT recoverable.

Calculate the corrected figure of VAT recoverable after making the adjustments below.

(i)   VAT of £237.00 on fuel scale charges has not yet been included.

(ii)   Bad debt relief on debts of £4,239.00 (VAT-inclusive) is to be claimed.

(iii) An invoice for a lorry purchase of £20,000 excluding VAT has not yet been included.

67 KYRA

Kyra makes a taxable supply of widgets at the standard rate. The value of the supply is £900.

A 2% bulk buy discount is offered due to the large quantity ordered on this occasion. A prompt payment discount of 5% is offered for payment within 30 days.

Assuming the prompt payment discount is taken, what is the VAT that Kyra must account for on this transaction. Choose one answer.

A   £180.00

B   £176.40

C   £171.00

D   £167.58

68 LARISSA

Larissa is a VAT-registered trader. She sells machine parts with a VAT-exclusive price of £750 to Exe Ltd.

She offers a prompt payment discount of 3% for customers who pay within 21 days.

(a) What is the correct amount of VAT to be shown on the invoice assuming Larissa adopts the policy of invoicing at the discounted amount? Choose one answer.

    A   £150.00

    B   £145.50

    C   £125.00

    D   £121.25

(b) If the customer pays after 21 days, what is the amount including VAT to be shown on the supplementary invoice to be issued to the customer?

Choose one answer.

    A   Nil

    B   £4.50

    C   £22.50

    D   £27.00

69 TRINA

Trina is a VAT-registered trader who makes a supply of automotive components for £240 to John which is a standard-rated supply.

Trina offers to pay her customer's VAT on their behalf. Accordingly, John pays £240 to Trina for some automotive parts.

What is the correct amount of VAT to be shown on the invoice?

    A   £48.00

    B   £40.00

70 NASHEEN

Nasheen is a VAT-registered trader who has made the following sales of standard-rated items in the previous month.

	£
To AB Ltd (amount inclusive of VAT)	562
To XY plc (amount exclusive of VAT)	750

What is the total output tax on these two supplies?

Select one option.

    A   £262.40

    B   £218.66

    C   £237.40

    D   £243.66

71 JULIE

Julie is a VAT-registered trader. During the last quarter she has made the following sales (all figures are exclusive of VAT).

	£
Standard-rated	40,145
Zero-rated	21,050
Exempt	3,450
Sale of used plant (Julie was registered when she purchased this plant)	5,000

How much output VAT should Julie account for in this quarter?

Select one option.

A   £7,524.16

B   £9,029.00

C   £13,239.00

D   £8,029.00

72 COMFY SOFAS LTD

Comfy Sofas Ltd normally sells sofas for £600 plus VAT of £120. They run a promotion where they offer to pay the customer's VAT. Fred buys a sofa and pays £600.

What is the VAT that Comfy Sofas Ltd must pay over?

£ _____

73 FINN

Finn's business makes a standard-rated supply of furniture. The VAT-exclusive value of the supply is £467.90 and a trade discount of 2% is offered.

What is the amount of VAT to be shown on the invoice correct to two decimal places?

£ _____

74 AMANDA

Amanda has completed her VAT account and the balance shows that she must pay VAT to HMRC. However, she has forgotten to make the entries listed in the table below.

For each, tick the appropriate box to indicate whether the amendment needed to the VAT account will increase, decrease or have no effect on the balance payable to HMRC.

	Increases balance payable to HMRC	Decreases balance payable to HMRC	No effect on balance payable to HMRC
VAT on purchases is understated			
Bad debt relief claim omitted			
Previous net over claim to be adjusted for on the VAT return omitted			
VAT on EU acquisition omitted			
Credit notes issued understated			
VAT on sales overstated			

75   ASHWIN

Ashwin has completed his VAT return for his latest quarter. It correctly shows VAT due to HMRC of £5,690.22.

The last quarter's VAT payment of £7,135.80 has been entered in the VAT account on the wrong side.

What is the **uncorrected** balance showing on the VAT account? Choose ONE answer.

A   £12,826.02 VAT due to HMRC

B   £19,961.82 VAT due to HMRC

C   £1,445.58 due from HMRC

D   £8,581.38 due from HMRC

76   REHMAN

Rehman has completed his VAT return for the last quarter. It correctly shows VAT due from HMRC of £1,768.50. The VAT account shows VAT due from HMRC of £2,488.00.

Which of the following explains the difference?

Choose ONE answer.

A   VAT of £359.75 on purchase invoices has been posted on the wrong side of the VAT account.

B   VAT of £719.50 on purchase invoices has been posted on the wrong side of the VAT account.

C   VAT of £359.75 on sales invoices has been posted to the wrong side of the VAT account.

D   VAT of £719.50 on sales invoices has been posted to the wrong side of the VAT account.

77 ANGELO

Angelo has received a purchase invoice. There is VAT included on the invoice but it is less than 20/120 of the total amount due.

Which of the following CANNOT be an explanation for this?

Choose ONE answer.

A   An error has been made in calculating the VAT

B   A trade discount is offered by the supplier

C   Angelo is a partially-exempt trader

D   Some of the supplies included on the invoice are zero-rated

78 ALYSSA

Alyssa runs an electrical retailing business. As part of a special promotion the business has offered to pay the VAT on all purchases of washing machines during the first week in May.

A customer buys a new washing machine on 3 May which normally sells for £487 + VAT. The customer pays £487 to Alyssa.

What is the amount of VAT to be accounted for by Alyssa correct to two decimal places?

£

79 HOLLY

Holly runs a VAT-registered business. She discovers the following non-careless, non-deliberate errors in the recording of VAT on sales invoices in her records.

(i)   VAT on an invoice to a customer recorded in June 20X1 shows output tax of £297.55 when it should have been £279.55.

(ii)   An invoice to another customer in July 20X1 shows output tax of £480.00 when it should have been £840.00.

The VAT return for the 3 months to 30 November 20X1 currently shows output tax of £3,556.40.

What would be the final figure for output tax on the VAT return for the quarter ended 30 November 20X1?

£

PREPARING SPECIFIC FIGURES FOR THE VAT RETURN

Key answer tips

Tasks in this area may have more than one part. The questions in this section of the kit give practice on the individual areas likely to be tested in this task.

In the tasks in this section of the kit, candidates are expected to perform some of the preparation work before compiling the VAT return. Not all of the figures needed for the full return are required, and there is always an adjusting value to work out and include in the calculations.

80   PATEL

Patel is a registered trader. He has written off the following debts on 30.9.X1:

Amount	Date of supply	Date payment due
£4,200	15.1.X1	28.1.X1
£6,552	6.3.X1	30.3.X1
£7,000	10.4.X1	30.3.X1
£2,500	7.5.X1	31.5.X1

All amounts are VAT-inclusive.

What is the total VAT irrecoverable (bad) debt relief that can be claimed in the quarter ended 30.9.X1?

£

81   JASPER

Jasper runs a UK business selling standard-rated golf accessories. He imports some items from overseas, both from other EU countries and from outside the EU. All purchases are items that would be standard-rated in the UK.

In the quarter ended 30 June 20X2 his purchases are as follows:

	£
Purchases from UK businesses	54,800
Purchases from EU registered businesses	27,400
Purchases from outside the EU	37,600

All these figures exclude VAT.

Complete Boxes 2, 4, 7 and 9 of the VAT return below.

		£
VAT due in the period on **sales** and other outputs	**Box 1**	
VAT due in the period on **acquisitions** from other **EU Member States**	**Box 2**	
Total VAT due (**the sum of boxes 1 and 2**)	**Box 3**	
VAT reclaimed in the period on **purchases** and other inputs, including acquisitions from the EU	**Box 4**	
Net VAT to be paid to HM Revenue & Customs or reclaimed (**Difference between boxes 3 and 4**)	**Box 5**	
Total value of **sales** and all other outputs excluding any VAT. **Include your box 8 figure**	**Box 6**	
Total value of purchases and all other inputs excluding any VAT. **Include your box 9 figure**	**Box 7**	
Total value of all **supplies** of goods and related costs, excluding any VAT, to other **EU Member States**	**Box 8**	
Total value of all **acquisitions** of goods and related costs, excluding any VAT, from other **EU Member States**	**Box 9**	

82 MISTRY

This task is about preparing figures for a VAT return for the period ended 31 March 20X0.

The business's EU acquisitions are goods that would normally be standard-rated.

The following accounts have been extracted from the business's ledgers:

Sales and sales returns account					
Date 20X0	Reference	Debit £	Date 20X0	Reference	Credit £
01/01 – 31/03	Sales returns day book – UK sales returns	9,000.00	01/01 – 31/03	Sales day book – UK sales	670,000.00
31/03	Balance c/d	759,200.00	01/01 – 31/03	Sales day book – EU despatches	98,200.00
	Total	**768,200.00**		**Total**	**768,200.00**

Purchases account					
Date 20X0	Reference	Debit £	Date 20X0	Reference	Credit £
01/01 – 31/03	Purchases day book – UK purchases	311,000.00	31/03	Balance c/d	360,000.00
01/01 – 31/03	Purchases day book – EU acquisitions	15,000.00			
01/01 – 31/03	Purchases day book – zero-rated imports	34,000.00			
	Total	**360,000.00**		**Total**	**360,000.00**

VAT account (Incomplete)					
Date 20X0	Reference	Debit £	Date 20X0	Reference	Credit £
01/01 – 31/03	Sales returns day book	1,800.00	01/01 – 31/03	Sales day book	134,000.00
01/01 – 31/03	Purchases day book	62,200.00			

EU despatches and acquisitions are with VAT-registered businesses.

(a) Calculate the figure for Box 2 of the VAT return – VAT due on acquisitions from other EU member states.

┌─────────────────────────────┐
│   │
└─────────────────────────────┘

(b) Calculate the figure for Box 1 of the VAT return – VAT due on sales and other outputs.

┌─────────────────────────────┐
│   │
└─────────────────────────────┘

(c) Calculate the figure for Box 4 of the VAT return – VAT reclaimed on purchases and other inputs, including acquisitions from the EU.

┌─────────────────────────────┐
│   │
└─────────────────────────────┘

83 FLETCH

This task is about preparing figures for a VAT return for the period ended 31 August 20X5.

The following accounts have been extracted from the business's ledgers:

	Purchases account				
Date 20X5	Reference	Debit £	Date 20X5	Reference	Credit £
01/06 – 31/08	Purchases day book – UK purchases	216,540.41	31/08	Balance c/d	235,080.03
01/06 – 31/08	Purchases day book – zero-rated imports	18,539.62			
	Total	235,080.03		Total	235,080.03

	VAT account				
Date 20X5	Reference	Debit £	Date 20X5	Reference	Credit £
01/06 – 31/08	Purchases day book – UK purchases	43,308.08	01/06 – 31/08	Sales day book – UK sales	20,265.67
			01/06 – 31/08	Cash book – UK sales	1,358.03

You are told that UK purchases included a van for £20,845 plus VAT and a company car for £30,607 plus VAT. The related VAT for both purchases is included in the VAT account figure.

(a) Calculate the figure for Box 1 of the VAT return – VAT due on sales and other outputs.

(b) Calculate the figure for Box 4 of the VAT return – VAT reclaimed on purchases and other inputs, including acquisitions from the EU.

(c) Calculate the figure for Box 7 of the VAT return – value of purchases and all other inputs, excluding any VAT, in whole pounds only.

84   HARDACRE

This task is about preparing figures for a VAT return for the period ended 30 June 20X0.

The following accounts have been extracted from the business's ledgers:

Sales account					
Date 20X0	Reference	Debit £	Date 20X0	Reference	Credit £
			01/04 – 30/06	Sales day book – UK sales	460,780.00
			01/04 – 30/06	Sales day book – exports	124,890.20
30/06	Balance c/d	631,570.20	01/04 – 30/06	Cash book – UK sales	45,900.00
	Total	**631,570.20**		**Total**	**631,570.20**

Purchases account					
Date 20X0	Reference	Debit £	Date 20X0	Reference	Credit £
01/04 – 30/06	Purchases day book – UK purchases	248,680.90	30/06	Balance c/d	283,353.20
01/04 – 30/06	Purchases day book – zero-rated imports	34,672.30			
	Total	**283,353.20**		**Total**	**283,353.20**

VAT account					
Date 20X0	Reference	Debit £	Date 20X0	Reference	Credit £
01/04 – 30/06	Purchases day book – UK purchases	49,736.18	01/04 – 30/06	Sales day book – UK sales	92,156.00
			01/04 – 30/06	Cash book – UK sales	9,180.00

You are told that irrecoverable debt relief on an invoice of £1,689.10 excluding VAT is to be claimed.

(a)   Calculate the figure to be reclaimed as irrecoverable debt relief on the VAT return.

```
┌────────────────────────────┐
│                            │
│                            │
└────────────────────────────┘
```

(b)   Calculate the figure for Box 1 of the VAT return – VAT due on sales and other outputs.

```
┌────────────────────────────┐
│                            │
│                            │
└────────────────────────────┘
```

(c)   Calculate the figure for Box 4 of the VAT return – VAT reclaimed on purchases and other inputs, including acquisitions from the EU.

```
┌────────────────────────────┐
│                            │
│                            │
└────────────────────────────┘
```

85   SPRINGER

This task is about preparing figures for a VAT return for the quarter to 31 December 20X3.

Springer is a sole trader whose business is registered for VAT. He does not use any special accounting schemes. All his sales and purchases are standard-rated for VAT.

He gives you the following information about transactions for the quarter to 31 December 20X3:

	£
Sales invoices issued for credit sales	67,800
Purchase invoices received from suppliers	45,350
Cash sales receipts	234
Sales credit notes issued	1,980
Purchase debit notes issued	2,100
Petty cash – purchases of standard-rated items	154

Irrecoverable (bad) debts of £2,496.66 (including VAT) have been written off in December 20X3. These debts refer to invoices due for payment in January 20X3.

All figures include VAT.

(a)   Calculate the figure for irrecoverable (bad) debt relief.

```



```

(b)   Calculate the figure for Box 3 of the VAT return – total VAT due.

```



```

(c)   Calculate the figure for Box 4 of the VAT return – VAT reclaimed on purchases and other inputs, including acquisitions from the EU.

```



```

86   JACOB

This task is about preparing figures for a VAT return for the period ended 30 June 20X8.

The business receives services from a supplier based in the EU. These are services that would normally be standard-rated. The net amount of the supply has been included in the purchases account but no other entry has been made.

The following accounts have been extracted from the business's ledgers:

Sales and sales returns account					
Date 20X8	Reference	Debit £	Date 20X8	Reference	Credit £
01/04 – 30/06	Sales returns day book – UK sales returns	4,000.00	01/04 – 30/06	Sales day book – UK sales	473,000.00
30/06	Balance c/d	504,400.00	01/04 – 30/06	Sales day book – EU despatches	35,400.00
	Total	508,400.00		**Total**	508,400.00

Purchases account					
Date 20X8	Reference	Debit £	Date 20X8	Reference	Credit £
01/04 – 30/06	Purchases day book – UK purchases	187,520.00	30/06	Balance c/d	202,694.00
01/04 – 30/06	Purchases day book – EU services	15,174.00			
	Total	202,694.00		**Total**	202,694.00

VAT account (Incomplete)					
Date 20X8	Reference	Debit £	Date 20X8	Reference	Credit £
01/04 – 30/06	Sales returns day book	800.00	01/04 – 30/06	Sales day book	94,600.00
01/04 – 30/06	Purchases day book	37,504.00			

EU despatches are to VAT-registered businesses.

(a)   Calculate the figure for Box 1 of the VAT return – VAT due in the period on sales and other outputs.

        _____

(b)   Calculate the figure for Box 4 of the VAT return – VAT reclaimed on purchases and other inputs, including acquisitions from the EU.

        _____

(c)   Calculate the figure for Box 6 of the VAT return – total value of sales and other outputs excluding any VAT. Provide your answer in whole pounds only.

        _____

COMPLETING AND SUBMITTING A VAT RETURN ACCURATELY

Key answer tips

The questions in this section of the kit give practice on completing VAT returns in full.

This is likely to be the most demanding task in an assessment with a much higher mark allocation than the other tasks. It requires the need to examine and analyse a lot of accounting data before working out the necessary statutory values and entering them in the right places, ready for completing the boxes on the VAT return and checking the values which the online return automatically generates.

87 DAVIES LTD

The following accounts have been extracted from a company's ledgers:

Date			Dr	Cr
			£	£
Purchases: UK				
31.3.X2	Purchases day book		69,200	
30.4.X2	Purchases day book		63,180	
31.5 X2	Purchases day book		67,340	
Sales: UK				
31.3.X2	Sales day book			121,000
30.4.X2	Sales day book			179,020
31.5 X2	Sales day book			140,800
Sales: Export EU				
31.3.X2	Sales day book			30,300
30.4.X2	Sales day book			41,160
31.5 X2	Sales day book			35,780
Sales: Exports non-EU				
31.3.X2	Sales day book			17,000
30.4.X2	Sales day book			14,900
31.5 X2	Sales day book			20,200
VAT: Output tax				
31.3.X2	Sales day book			24,200
30.4.X2	Sales day book			35,804
31.5 X2	Sales day book			28,160
VAT: Input tax				
31.3.X2	Purchases day book		13,840	
30.4.X2	Purchases day book		12,636	
31.5 X2	Purchases day book		13,468	

You are given the following further information.

1   VAT returns are completed quarterly and submitted electronically.

2   All EU exports are to VAT-registered customers.

3   Payments are made by electronic bank transfer.

4   An error was made in the previous return. Input tax was over claimed by £5,450.95.

5   Today's date is 19 June 20X2.

Complete Boxes 1 to 9 of the following VAT return for the quarter ended 31 May 20X2.

		£
VAT due in the period on **sales** and other outputs	**Box 1**	
VAT due in the period on **acquisitions** from other **EU Member States**	**Box 2**	
Total VAT due (**the sum of boxes 1 and 2**)	**Box 3**	
VAT reclaimed in the period on **purchases** and other inputs, including acquisitions from the EU	**Box 4**	
Net VAT to be paid to HM Revenue & Customs or reclaimed (**Difference between boxes 3 and 4**)	**Box 5**	
Total value of **sales** and all other outputs excluding any VAT. **Include your box 8 figure**	**Box 6**	
Total value of purchases and all other inputs excluding any VAT. **Include your box 9 figure**	**Box 7**	
Total value of all **supplies** of goods and related costs, excluding any VAT, to other **EU Member States**	**Box 8**	
Total value of all **acquisitions** of goods and related costs, excluding any VAT, from other **EU Member States**	**Box 9**	

88   TROTT

From the summarised day books below, complete the VAT return for the quarter to 31 March 20X5.

Trott does not use any special VAT accounting scheme.

Sales day book

		Total	VAT	UK sales
		£	£	£
Total	31 March 20X5	8,820.00	1,470.00	7,350.00

Sales credit notes day book

		Total	VAT	UK sales
		£	£	£
Total	31 March 20X5	420.00	70.00	350.00

Purchase day book

		Total	VAT	Purchases	Other expenses
		£	£	£	£
Total	31 March 20X5	4,332.00	722.00	2,160.00	1,450.00

Cash receipts book

		Total	VAT	Cash sales	Cash from debtors
		£	£	£	£
Total	31 March 20X5	5,092.00	52.00	260.00	4,780.00

Cash payments book

		Total	VAT	Cash purchases	Pay to creditors
		£	£	£	£
Total	31 March 20X5	4,230.00	30.00	150.00	4,050.00

Petty cash book

		Total	VAT	Sundry
		£	£	£
Total	31 March 20X5	198.00	33.00	165.00

Trott gives you the following additional information:

Trott has written off as an irrecoverable (bad) debt an amount of £235 (including VAT) which was due for payment 8 months before.

On 30 March he purchased a car for £7,920 (including VAT) which he will use for business and private use. This car has not yet been recorded in the accounting records.

		£
VAT due in the period on **sales** and other outputs	**Box 1**	
VAT due in the period on **acquisitions** from other **EC Member States**	**Box 2**	
Total VAT due (**the sum of boxes 1 and 2**)	**Box 3**	
VAT reclaimed in the period on **purchases** and other inputs, including acquisitions from the EC	**Box 4**	
Net VAT to be paid to HM Revenue & Customs or reclaimed (**Difference between boxes 3 and 4**)	**Box 5**	
Total value of **sales** and all other outputs excluding any VAT. **Include your box 8 figure**	**Box 6**	
Total value of purchases and all other inputs excluding any VAT. **Include your box 9 figure**	**Box 7**	
Total value of all **supplies** of goods and related costs, excluding any VAT, to other **EC Member States**	**Box 8**	
Total value of all **acquisitions** of goods and related costs, excluding any VAT, from other **EC Member States**	**Box 9**	

89   BARTLET LTD

Complete the VAT return given using the information below which is taken from the summarised day books and petty cash book for the quarter ended 30 September 20X2.

	Net £.pp	VAT £.pp	Total £.pp
Sales day book			
UK standard-rated sales	20,500.00	4,100.00	24,600.00
UK zero-rated sales	13,470.00	Nil	13,470.00
UK exempt sales	1,650.00	N/A	1,650.00
Sales to VAT-registered EU customers	5,105.00	Nil	5,105.00
Sales to non VAT-registered EU customers	1,200.00	240.00	1,440.00
Exports outside the EU	3,750.00	Nil	3,750.00
Purchases day book			
UK purchases and expenses	17,000.00	3,400.00	20,400.00
Purchases from EU businesses	2,860.00	572.00	3,432.00
Petty cash book			
UK purchases and expenses	640.00	128.00	768.00

Notes:

(i)   The business has no cash sales or purchases recorded in the cash books.

(ii)   No partial exemption adjustment is required.

(iii)   The business files returns quarterly and uses electronic filing and payment.

(iv)   As well as the purchases above, the business has incurred wages costs of £5,600 in the quarter.

(v)   Assume the date is 20 October 20X2.

		£
VAT due in the period on **sales** and other outputs	Box 1	
VAT due in the period on **acquisitions** from other **EU Member States**	Box 2	
Total VAT due (**the sum of boxes 1 and 2**)	Box 3	
VAT reclaimed in the period on **purchases** and other inputs, including acquisitions from the EU	Box 4	
Net VAT to be paid to HM Revenue & Customs or reclaimed (**Difference between boxes 3 and 4**)	Box 5	
Total value of **sales** and all other outputs excluding any VAT. **Include your box 8 figure**	Box 6	
Total value of purchases and all other inputs excluding any VAT. **Include your box 9 figure**	Box 7	
Total value of all **supplies** of goods and related costs, excluding any VAT, to other **EU Member States**	Box 8	
Total value of all **acquisitions** of goods and related costs, excluding any VAT, from other **EU Member States**	Box 9	

90   O'BRIEN

This task consists of preparing a VAT return for the period ended 30 June 20X0.

The following accounts have been extracted from the business's ledgers:

Date 20X0	Reference	Debit £	Date 20X0	Reference	Credit £
				Sales account	
			01/04 – 30/06	Sales daybook – UK sales	689,555.72
			01/04 – 30/06	Sales daybook – exports	81,560.00
30/06	Balance c/d	803,794.62	01/04 – 30/06	Cash book – UK sales	32,678.90
	Total	803,794.62		**Total**	803,794.62

Date 20X0	Reference	Debit £	Date 20X0	Reference	Credit £
				Purchases account	
01/04 – 30/06	Purchases day book – UK purchases	513,940.85	30/06	Balance c/d	545,629.45
01/04 – 30/06	Purchases daybook – EU acquisitions	31,688.60			
	Total	545,629.45		**Total**	545,629.45

Date 20X0	Reference	Debit £	Date 20X0	Reference	Credit £
				VAT account	
01/04 – 30/06	Purchases daybook – UK purchases	102,788.17	01/04 – 30/06	Sales daybook – UK sales	137,911.14
			01/04 – 30/06	Cash book – UK sales	6,535.78

You are told that the VAT on EU acquisitions is £6,337.72.

O'Brien has also received services from a VAT-registered business within the EU costing £24,700. No VAT was charged on this supply although the services would be standard-rated if purchased within the UK. O'Brien has not yet recorded this purchase in the ledgers.

Prepare the VAT return using the information above.

		£
VAT due in the period on **sales** and other outputs	**Box 1**	
VAT due in the period on **acquisitions** from other **EU Member States**	**Box 2**	
Total VAT due (**the sum of boxes 1 and 2**)	**Box 3**	
VAT reclaimed in the period on **purchases** and other inputs, including acquisitions from the EU	**Box 4**	
Net VAT to be paid to HM Revenue & Customs or reclaimed (**Difference between boxes 3 and 4**)	**Box 5**	
Total value of **sales** and all other outputs excluding any VAT. **Include your box 8 figure**	**Box 6**	
Total value of purchases and all other inputs excluding any VAT. **Include your box 9 figure**	**Box 7**	
Total value of all **supplies** of goods and related costs, excluding any VAT, to other **EU Member States**	**Box 8**	
Total value of all **acquisitions** of goods and related costs, excluding any VAT, from other **EU Member States**	**Box 9**	

91   STEWART LTD (1)

The following balances have been extracted from a company's ledgers at the end of the quarter to 31 October 20X5:

	Dr	Cr
	£	£
Purchases – UK	59,678	
Purchases – EU businesses	14,593	
Purchase credit notes – UK		2,569
Expenses (all standard-rated)	19,437	
Wages and salaries	8,750	
Sales – UK		145,450
Sales credit notes	3,568	
VAT – input tax on UK purchases and expenses	15,309.20	
VAT – output tax on UK sales		28,376.40

Notes:

(i) The financial accountant is aware that the company needs to do something about VAT on the purchases from EU businesses but no entries have been made in the ledger for the VAT on these yet.

(ii) Stewart Ltd also has received the following invoice, which relates to the quarter ended 31 October 20X5, but which has not yet been included in the records.

	Gross	VAT	Net
	£	£	£
Purchase of a lorry	24,000.00	4,000.00	20,000.00

(iii) The company files its VAT returns and pays its VAT electronically.

Prepare the VAT return for the quarter ended 31 October 20X5.

		£
VAT due in the period on **sales** and other outputs	Box 1	
VAT due in the period on **acquisitions** from other **EC Member States**	Box 2	
Total VAT due (**the sum of boxes 1 and 2**)	Box 3	
VAT reclaimed in the period on **purchases** and other inputs, including acquisitions from the EC	Box 4	
Net VAT to be paid to HM Revenue & Customs or reclaimed (**Difference between boxes 3 and 4**)	Box 5	
Total value of **sales** and all other outputs excluding any VAT. **Include your box 8 figure**	Box 6	
Total value of purchases and all other inputs excluding any VAT. **Include your box 9 figure**	Box 7	
Total value of all **supplies** of goods and related costs, excluding any VAT, to other **EC Member States**	Box 8	
Total value of all **acquisitions** of goods and related costs, excluding any VAT, from other **EC Member States**	Box 9	

COMMUNICATING VAT INFORMATION

Key answer tips

The questions in this section of the kit give practice on the types of question which may be tested in the assessment.

These tasks tests a candidate's ability to communicate with others and to absorb accurately the data given to them before completing the exercise.

92   STEWART LTD (2)

Refer to the information in Stewart Ltd (1) above.

Since receiving the information above you have discovered that the lorry was not in fact delivered or invoiced until after 31 October. The financial accountant suggests that it is too much trouble to make an adjustment if it is deemed necessary.

Complete the following email to the financial accountant about the capital expenditure in the period and the date the return will be due.

For words in bold, select the correct word/phrase. Today's date is 17 November 20X5.

Email

To:

From:

Date:

Subject:

Please be advised that I have just completed the VAT return for the quarter ended (............................).

The amount of VAT **(payable/receivable)** will be (£................................).

The return must be with HMRC on or before (........................).

The VAT will be **(paid electronically by ..../received directly into our bank account)**.

I **have/have not** included the invoice for capital expenditure. VAT of (£.................) **can/cannot** be reclaimed on this expenditure in the current quarter.

Kind regards

---

93 DHONI LTD

You are an accounting technician who has prepared the VAT return for Dhoni Ltd for the quarter ended 31 December 20X2.

Today's date is 17 January 20X3.

In the previous quarter output VAT was understated by £4,672.90. In the current quarter the figure from Box 6 of the return is £210,050.

Complete the following email to the financial accountant explaining whether the error can be corrected on the VAT return to 31 December 20X2.

For words in bold, select the correct word/phrase.

Email

To:

From:

Date:

Subject:

An error occurred in the VAT return for the previous quarter. Output VAT of £4,672.90 was **(over/understated)**. This resulted in VAT being **(over/under paid)**.

This error **(was included on the VAT return to 31 December/must be separately notified to HMRC)**.

Kind regards

---

94 BELL

You are an accounting technician working for a firm of accountants. You have just completed the VAT return for the quarter to 31 March 20X5 for one of your clients, Andrew Bell.

Andrew Bell wrote off a debt of £6,467 on 28 February 20X5. This debt had been outstanding since 15 August 20X4.

Complete the following email to Bell explaining how you have dealt with the irrecoverable (bad) debt.

For words in bold, select the correct word/phrase. The date is 17 April 20X5.

Email

To:

From:

Date:

Subject:

Thank you for advising me about the debt you wrote off. I have included relief for this in the VAT return for the quarter ended (………………………………………….).

Relief can be claimed because the debt was due for payment more than (**3 months/ 6 months**) ago.

The (**input/output**) tax paid on the original invoice can be reclaimed by including the amount in (**Box 1/Box 4**). The amount of irrecoverable (bad) debt relief is (£…………………).

Kind regards

---

95   SEABORN LTD

Seaborn Ltd is a new company that has just registered for VAT.

It makes mainly standard-rated supplies with a few zero-rated supplies. It does not use any special accounting schemes.

You are an accounting technician. Today's date is 5 September 20X6.

Complete the following email to the financial accountant advising generally when VAT returns must be filed. For words in bold, select the correct word/phrase.

Email

To:

From:

Date:

Subject:

VAT returns must be submitted (**monthly/quarterly/yearly**) unless you are a net repayment trader when returns can be made (**monthly/quarterly/yearly**).

Returns must be filed within (**30 days/1 month/3 months**) after the end of the VAT period with an extension of (**3 days/7 days/2 weeks**) where returns are filed online.

You (**have a choice as to whether you file returns on paper or online/must file online**).

Kind regards

---

96 MILES LTD

You are an accounts assistant working for Miles Ltd. From 1 September 20X2 the company's main product is changing from being zero-rated to standard-rated.

Complete the following email to be circulated to the Miles Ltd sales and sales invoicing staff. For words in bold, select the correct word/phrase.

Today's date is 14 July 20X2.

Email

To:

From:

Date:

Subject: Change in VAT treatment

As you know the company's main product has been reclassified from one that is (**zero-rated/standard-rated**) to one that is (**zero-rated/standard-rated**).

All sales invoices (**issued on or after 1 September/with a tax point on or after 1 September**) must have the standard rate of VAT applied.

As we have decided to keep our VAT-inclusive prices the same, the price of goods to our customers will (**increase/decrease/stay the same**) and our profits will (**increase/decrease/ stay the same**).

Kind regards

---

97 ELSIE

You are employed by Elsie as an accounts assistant. Your supervisor is Abed.

You have only been working for a week and you are due to have training to learn how to deal with VAT accounting on areas that are completely new to you.

Unfortunately Abed is very busy and has no time to train you before the VAT return is due.

Abed says 'This return is due in 2 days. Just guess the bits you are not sure about'.

Which of the following would be a suitable course of action?

A   You are a bit nervous about bothering your supervisor so you do prepare the return and guess the bits you do not know.

B   You research the areas of which you are unsure. Although you are still not happy with all areas you go ahead and prepare the return.

C   You research the areas of which you are unsure and refer your remaining queries to Abed.

Section 2

ANSWERS TO PRACTICE QUESTIONS

FINDING OUT ABOUT VAT, REGISTRATION, VAT RECORDS

Key answer tips

The chief assessor has said in the past that the most common reason for being not yet competent in registration tasks was a lack of knowledge of the registration rules, particularly the 'future prospects' rule for registration.

Candidates need to look more carefully at the figures supplied in the task and remember that a business can voluntarily register at any time: they do not have to be close to the threshold in order to do so.

Some candidates had issues with record tasks and it was surprising the number who felt that estimates and pro-formas were records which had to be kept.

Some did not know that VAT is a tax which is only suffered by the unregistered end purchaser, mainly the public, because all other parties in the chain of events which take goods from manufacturers to final sale to consumers can claim back any VAT they have been charged along the way.

1 HUSSEY

(a) The answer is B

The historic registration test is based on a business exceeding £85,000 of taxable turnover in the last 12 months or since starting in business if this is less than 12 months. Taxable turnover excludes exempt supplies and for registration purposes it also excludes the sale of capital assets.

In A the business has only £43,100 of taxable turnover and in D it has none.

A business that only makes zero-rated sales can choose to claim exemption from registration when it has more than £85,000 of taxable turnover. C is therefore not **required** to **be** registered.

(b) The answer is C

Key answer tips

Information about this topic is included in the indirect tax reference material provided in the assessment, so you do not need to learn it.

However you need to be familiar with its location and content – why not look at it now?

2   HUGH

The answer is B

Statement (i) is false as Hugh would have to be expecting taxable supplies of less than the deregistration threshold of £83,000 in the next 12 months to avoid having to register now.

Statement (ii) is true. Sales of capital assets are not included in the total of taxable supplies for registration purposes. Hence the business has made only £76,000 of relevant taxable supplies and as this is less than the registration threshold of £85,000, the business does not need to register.

Statement (iii) is true. Businesses must notify HMRC within 30 days of the end of the month in which the registration threshold is exceeded and will be registered from the start of the month which starts one month after exceeding the threshold.

Statement (iv) is largely correct but the business will be registered with effect from the **start** of the 30 day period, not the end.

Key answer tips

Make sure you read written questions like this thoroughly.

Part (iv) looks correct at first reading. You have to look at it carefully to notice the error.

3   JENKINS

The answer is B

Individuals have one registration covering all their sole trader businesses but not those they run in partnership with others.

The two partnerships must be separately registered.

This makes 3 registrations in total.

Tutorial note

A sole trader has a single registration covering all the businesses they run as a sole trader. So it is the combined turnover of all their businesses that must be checked to see if it is over the registration threshold. In this case Jenkins has £120,000 from his sole trader businesses and must register.

*Separate partnerships, but with the same partners, must also have a single registration, so if Jenkins and **only** his wife ran another business in partnership they would have to include that in their partnership registration.*

Companies are individually registered.

4   NASSER

(a)   Voluntary registration

	Would not voluntarily register
It makes their goods more expensive for other VAT-registered businesses.	
It makes their goods more expensive for businesses that are not VAT-registered.	✓
It helps to avoid penalties for late registration.	
It increases the business burden of administration.	✓

Tutorial note

Voluntary registration is open to all businesses that make, or intend to make, taxable supplies.

Voluntary registration is useful because:

1   It avoids the possibility of penalties for late registration.

2   It disguises the small size of the business.

3   It is useful for businesses that sell zero-rated goods to register as they can still reclaim input VAT (VAT on purchases).

Disadvantages of voluntary registration include:

1   It increases the burden of administration for small businesses.

2   It causes the sales price of goods to be increased by the addition of VAT. This is only a problem for those, like the public, who cannot recover VAT. Other VAT-registered businesses can recover the VAT so they would not be affected if the business voluntarily registered for VAT.

A person may consider not voluntarily registering if they will suffer the disadvantages above (i.e. increased administrative burden and if they have customers that are not VAT-registered).

(b)   The answer is D

5 **ISY**

(a) The answer is C

Taxable turnover is £8,000 per month and after 11 months, at the end of October, the business will have made £88,000 of taxable supplies.

Tutorial note

The historic registration test is based on a business exceeding £85,000 of taxable turnover in the last 12 months or since starting in business if this is less than 12 months. Taxable turnover excludes exempt supplies but includes zero-rated supplies.

(b) The answer is YES

Key answer tips

Information about this topic is included in the indirect tax reference material provided in the assessment, so you do not need to learn it.

However you need to be familiar with its location and content – why not look at it now?

6 **VOLUNTARY DEREGISTRATION**

	Yes	No
A business which is ceasing to trade.		✓
A continuing business which expects to make supplies of £83,000 in the next year of which one quarter will be exempt supplies.	✓	
A business which expects to make taxable supplies of £84,000 in the next 12 months.		✓
A continuing business which has been making taxable supplies of £87,000 per year but which has now switched to making wholly exempt supplies of the same amount.		✓

Tutorial note

A business can deregister if they wish to, if it is expected taxable turnover for the next 12 months is below the deregistration threshold (currently £83,000).

A business which has ceased to trade or which switches to making wholly exempt supplies MUST deregister. They cannot deregister voluntarily.

In the example above, only the second business can deregister voluntarily. They are expecting to make taxable supplies in the next 12 months of £62,250 which is below the deregistration threshold.

Key answer tips

Information about this topic is included in the indirect tax reference material provided in the assessment, so you do not need to learn it.

However you need to be familiar with its location and content – why not look at it now?

7   DOOKU

	Register now	Monitor & register later
A business with £50,000 of taxable turnover in the last 11 months but which expects taxable turnover of £87,000 in the next 30 days.	✓	
A business with taxable turnover of £5,000 per month for last 12 months.		✓
A business with taxable turnover of £7,500 per month for the last 12 months.	✓	
A business with turnover of standard-rated supplies of £4,000 per month for the last year but which expects turnover of £50,000 in the next 30 days.		✓

Tutorial note

Under the historic registration test a business must register if it has in excess of £85,000 of taxable turnover in the last 12 months or since starting in business if this is less than 12 months.

Under the future turnover test a business must register if taxable turnover of more than the registration threshold is expected in the next 30 days.

The first business has to register under the future test as they are expecting £87,000 of turnover in the next 30 days and the third business under the historic test (12 months × £7,500 = £90,000).

Key answer tips

Information about this topic is included in the indirect tax reference material provided in the assessment, so you do not need to learn it.

However you need to be familiar with its location and content – why not look at it now?

8   CERTIFICATE OF REGISTRATION

(a)   The answer is C

(b)   HMRC powers

	Is a power	Is not a power
Charging penalties for breaches of VAT rules	✓	
Completing VAT returns		✓
Inspecting premises	✓	
Providing suitable books for VAT record keeping		✓
Changing the rate of VAT		✓

Tutorial note

The certificate of registration proves that a business is registered for VAT. It shows the VAT registration number which must be shown on their invoices.

The rate of VAT is changed by legislative procedure, not unilaterally by HMRC.

9   REMONA

The answer is C

A is incorrect because the £15,000 of turnover will be treated as VAT-inclusive. VAT of £2,500.00 (£15,000 × 1/6) will be payable.

B is incorrect as the turnover for the historic test must be measured at the end of a month.

D is incorrect as some businesses (e.g. ones making zero-rated supplies) have monthly returns and under the annual accounting scheme businesses just have one yearly return.

10   RHYS

The answer is C

A business making taxable supplies below the registration threshold (whether or not they are making exempt supplies) is not required to register but may register voluntarily.

Zero-rated supplies are taxable supplies.

The other statements are true.

11 TROI

The answer is B

Working: Cumulative taxable turnover for the last 12 months

		£
End Dec 20X5	(£6,000 × 12)	72,000
End Jan 20X6	(£72,000 + £5,600 Jan X6 – £6,000 Jan X5))	71,600
End Feb 20X6	(£71,600 + £11,100 Feb X6 – £6,000 Feb X5)	76,700
End Mar 20X6	(£76,700 + £15,100 Mar X6 – £6,000 Mar X5)	85,800

Tutorial note

The historic registration test is based on a business exceeding £85,000 of taxable turnover in the last 12 months or since starting in business if this is less than 12 months. Taxable turnover excludes exempt supplies but includes zero-rated supplies.

12 BARCLAY

The answer is D

Evading VAT is a criminal offence so this is not a good reason to keep up-to-date.

13 LO

	True	False
Businesses must keep records of all taxable and exempt supplies made in the course of business.	✓	
Taxpayers need permission from HMRC before they start keeping records electronically.		✓
All businesses must keep a VAT account.	✓	
The balance on the VAT account represents the VAT payable to HMRC or repayable by HMRC.	✓	
Sending or receiving invoices by electronic means is permitted but paper copies must also be kept.		✓
Records should normally be kept for at least 3 years before being destroyed.		✓
Failure to keep records can lead to a penalty.	✓	

Tutorial note

Records should be kept for 6 years. Records include purchases, purchase returns day book, sales, sales returns day book, cashbook, invoices, credit notes, delivery notes, bank statements and the VAT summary (ledger account).

Key answer tips

Information about this topic is included in the indirect tax reference material provided in the assessment, so you do not need to learn it.

However you need to be familiar with its location and content – why not look at it now?

VAT INVOICES, TAX POINT, MAKING EXEMPT SUPPLIES

Key answer tips

The chief assessor has said in the past that the most common reason for being not yet competent in questions on these areas was as follows: poor skills in applying knowledge of tax points and the time limits for issuing VAT invoices.

Identifying the correct tax point and the problem of invoice issue deadlines are crucial to knowing the right VAT return on which to report inputs and outputs, and as such it is a critical area of compliance.

14   CAIN

(a)   The answer is C

(b)   The answer is B

(c)   The answer is B

Tutorial note

The basic tax point is the date of delivery of goods or the date of performance of services. This is the case with (c).

However, if goods or services are paid for in advance or a tax invoice is issued in advance, the date of payment or the invoice date becomes the tax point date. This is the case with (b). The basic tax point is 24 August (i.e. date the goods are delivered). However, the actual tax point date is the date payment is received, as payment is received before the basic tax point date.

Note that a pro-forma invoice is raised before the payment date. However, a pro-forma invoice is not a VAT invoice. Even if a valid VAT invoice had been raised on 17 August, it was not sent to the customer until after the goods were delivered. To issue a VAT invoice it must be sent to, or given to, the customer for them to keep. A tax point cannot be created simply by preparing an invoice.

Where goods are not paid for or invoiced in advance, a later tax point can arise if a tax invoice is raised within 14 days after the basic tax point. This is the case with (a). This is referred to as the '14 day rule'. The basic tax point date is 15 May (i.e. date the goods are delivered). However, the actual tax point date is the invoice date as the valid invoice is issued and sent on 20 May (i.e. within 14 days of 15 May).

Taxpayers can also apply to HMRC for a tax point date to fit in with their invoicing routine.

Key answer tips

Information about this topic is included in the indirect tax reference material provided in the assessment, so you do not need to learn it.

However you need to be familiar with its location and content – why not look at it now?

15 RATTAN

(a) The answer is B

(b) The answer is C

(c) The answer is A

Tutorial note

The basic tax point is the date of delivery of goods or the date of performance of services. This is the case with (a).

However, if goods or services are paid for in advance or a tax invoice is issued in advance, the date of payment or the invoice date becomes the tax point date. This is the case with (c). The tax point date in respect of the deposit is the date payment is received.

Where goods are not paid for or invoiced in advance, a later tax point can arise if a tax invoice is raised within 14 days after the basic tax point. This is the case with (b). This is referred to as the '14 day rule'.

Taxpayers can also apply to HMRC for a tax point date to fit in with their invoicing routine.

Key answer tips

Information about this topic is included in the indirect tax reference material provided in the assessment, so you do not need to learn it.

However you need to be familiar with its location and content – why not look at it now?

16   ROGER

Deposit paid	Goods delivered	Invoice raised	Balance paid	Tax point for deposit	Tax point for balance
10 March	12 March	30 March	18 March	**10 March**	**12 March** (Delivery date)
21 February	7 March	10 March	1 April	**21 February**	**10 March** (14 day rule)
13 May	26 May	11 June	7 July	**13 May**	**26 May** (Delivery date)

Tutorial note

The basic tax point is the date of delivery of goods or the date of performance of services.

However, if goods or services are paid for in advance or a tax invoice is issued in advance, the date of payment or the invoice date becomes the tax point date.

If a part payment such as a deposit is paid in advance then there will be two tax points, one for the deposit and one for the balance of the supply.

Where goods are not paid for or invoiced in advance, a later tax point can arise if a tax invoice is raised within 14 days after the basic tax point. This is referred to as the '14 day rule'.

Key answer tips

Information about this topic is included in the indirect tax reference material provided in the assessment, so you do not need to learn it.

However you need to be familiar with its location and content – why not look at it now?

17   BOLD

(a)   Zero-rated supply invoices

	True	False
The tax point date is 20 July.	✓	
The tax point date is 25 July.		✓
An invoice for a wholly zero-rated supply is not a tax invoice.	✓	
Input tax recovery in respect of zero-rated supplies is restricted.		✓

Tutorial note

An invoice for a wholly zero-rated supply within the UK is not a tax invoice. Hence the 14 day rule cannot apply. The tax point date will be the earlier of the receipt of cash or the despatch of goods.

*However, zero-rated supplies **are** taxable supplies and any input tax incurred in helping to make zero-rated goods or perform zero-rated services is fully recoverable.*

Key answer tips

Information about this topic is included in the indirect tax reference material provided in the assessment, so you do not need to learn it.

However you need to be familiar with its location and content – why not look at it now?

(b)   The answer is C

It is not a valid simplified invoice as the value of the supply exceeds £250.

There is insufficient detail for it to be a valid full invoice.

18   RANKIN

Deposit paid	Goods delivered	Invoice raised	Balance paid	Tax point for deposit	Tax point for balance
28 June	14 July	17 July	5 August	**28 June**	**17 July** (14 day rule)
19 October	31 October	16 November	12 December	**19 October**	**31 October** (Delivery date)
2 December	4 December	22 December	10 December	**2 December**	**4 December** (Delivery date)

Tutorial note

The basic tax point is the date of delivery of goods or the date of performance of services.

However, if goods or services are paid for in advance or a tax invoice is issued in advance, the date of payment or the invoice date becomes the tax point date. If a part payment such as a deposit is paid in advance then there will be two tax points, one for the deposit and one for the balance of the supply.

Where goods are not paid for or invoiced in advance, a later tax point can arise if a tax invoice is raised within 14 days after the basic tax point. This is referred to as the '14 day rule'.

Key answer tips

Information about this topic is included in the indirect tax reference material provided in the assessment, so you do not need to learn it.

However you need to be familiar with its location and content – why not look at it now?

19 MARGARET

(a) The answer is D

A supplier credit note means a purchase credit note. VAT on purchase credit notes is deducted from input VAT on purchase invoices so input tax will decrease.

(b) The answer is B

Sales to EU VAT-registered customers are zero-rated so there will be no effect on output or input VAT.

20 MARGOT

	True	False
The receipt of a credit note from a supplier will reduce her output tax.		✓
The issue of a debit note to a supplier will reduce her input tax.	✓	
The issue of a credit note to a customer will reduce her output tax.	✓	
The receipt of a debit note from a customer will reduce her output tax.	✓	

Tutorial note

Sales credit notes issued to customers are deducted from sales invoices and hence reduce the amount of output tax.

Purchase debit notes issued to suppliers are deducted from purchase invoices and hence reduce the amount of input tax.

A credit note from a supplier relates to purchases from that supplier. It is deducted from purchase invoices and hence reduces the amount of input tax.

A debit note from a customer relates to sales to that customer. It is deducted from sales invoices and hence reduces the amount of output tax.

21   JONSSON

(a)   The answer is C

(b)   The answer is D

Key answer tips

Information about this topic is included in the indirect tax reference material provided in the assessment, so you do not need to learn it.

However you need to be familiar with its location and content – why not look at it now?

22   AHMED

	Required	Not required
Time of supply	✓	
Customer order number		✓
Description of the type of supply	✓	
Rate of VAT applicable	✓	
General terms of trade		✓
Total amount payable excluding VAT	✓	
Total amount of VAT payable	✓	
Acceptable methods of payment		✓

Tutorial note

VAT invoices should contain the following:

1   *Identifying number which must follow a sequence*

2   *Date of supply (or tax point) and the date of issue of the invoice*

3   *Supplier's name and address and registration number*

4   *Name and address of customer (i.e. the person to whom the goods or services are supplied)*

5   *Type of supply (e.g. sale, hire purchase, exchange etc.)*

6   *Description of the goods or service*

7   *Quantity of goods or extent of service for each separate description*

8   *Unit price, rate of tax and amount payable (in sterling) excluding VAT for each separate description*

9   *Rate of any discount offered*

10   *Total amount of VAT chargeable.*

> *Simplified invoices need to show:*
>
> 1   *Date of supply*
>
> 2   *Supplier's name and address and registration number*
>
> 3   *Description of the goods or service*
>
> 4   *Rate of tax and amount payable (in sterling) including VAT for each separate rate of VAT.*

Key answer tips

Information about this topic is included in the indirect tax reference material provided in the assessment, so you do not need to learn it.

However you need to be familiar with its location and content – why not look at it now?

23   NERISSA

	True	False
Pro-forma invoices must show the VAT registration number of the supplier.		✓
Pro-forma invoices are a way of obtaining payment before goods are despatched.	✓	
The purchaser can use a pro-forma invoice to recover input VAT.		✓

Tutorial note

*To help with cash flow, a business may issue a **pro-forma invoice** which essentially is a demand for payment. Once payment is received, the business will then issue a 'live' invoice to replace the pro-forma.*

Because a pro-forma invoice does not rank as a VAT invoice the supplier is not required to pay VAT to HMRC until the 'live' invoice is issued. For this reason, the customer cannot reclaim VAT on a pro-forma invoice but must instead wait until the valid VAT invoice is received.

*Pro-forma invoices must be clearly marked with the words **'This is not a VAT invoice'**.*

24 CHEN

(a) The answer is D

(b) The answer is B

Tutorial note

Sales credit notes are deducted from sales invoices and hence reduce the amount of output tax.

A supplier credit note is a purchase credit note. It is deducted from purchase invoices and hence reduces the amount of input tax. If input tax decreases, the amount of tax due to HMRC will increase.

25 EFFIE

(a) The answer is D

(b) The answer is B

Tutorial note

Retailers selling to the public do not need to issue a tax invoice to a customer unless they request one.

Any business can issue a simplified (less detailed) tax invoice provided the total amount (including VAT) does not exceed £250.

Retailers do not need to keep copies of less detailed invoices. This is because retailers usually determine their VAT from sales records like till rolls rather than from a sales day book listing of invoices.

Key answer tips

Information about this topic is included in the indirect tax reference material provided in the assessment, so you do not need to learn it.

However you need to be familiar with its location and content – why not look at it now?

26   PUCK

The answer is C

Tutorial note

For a partially-exempt trader, input tax suffered by a business has to be split between that relating to taxable and to exempt supplies. Overhead costs which do not relate directly to taxable or exempt supplies are apportioned.

Input tax suffered on goods and services used to create exempt supplies cannot normally be recovered. However, if the de minimis limits are not exceeded, all of the input VAT can be recovered.

27   JERRY

	True	False
Traders who make only exempt supplies cannot register for VAT.	✓	
Traders who only make zero-rated supplies have to register for VAT.		✓
Zero-rated supplies made by a registered trader are not classed as taxable supplies.		✓
Traders making only exempt supplies cannot recover input tax.	✓	
VAT-registered traders making a mix of zero-rated and exempt supplies cannot recover any input tax.		✓

Tutorial note

In order to register for VAT, a trader must be making or intending to make taxable supplies. Exempt supplies are not taxable supplies, so traders making only exempt supplies cannot register and cannot recover input tax.

Traders making only zero-rated supplies can register, as zero-rated supplies are taxable supplies. Such traders can also choose not to register if they wish to avoid the administration burden of dealing with VAT. However, they cannot reclaim input tax if they do not register.

Traders making a mix of zero-rated and exempt supplies can recover a proportion of their input tax. They can recover all their input tax provided that the input tax which relates to making exempt supplies does not exceed a 'de minimis' amount.

28   SALLY

	Can be issued	Cannot be issued
Standard-rated supplies of £210		✓
Standard-rated supplies of £170 plus zero-rated supplies of £40	✓	
Standard-rated supplies of £170 plus exempt supplies of £40		✓

Tutorial note

A simplified invoice may be issued if the total of the invoice **including** VAT is £250 or less.

The first invoice will attract VAT of £42 (£210 × 20%) making a total of £252 which exceeds the limit.

The second invoice will attract VAT of £34 (£170 × 20%) making a total of £244 which is below the limit.

Exempt supplies must not be included on a simplified invoice.

29 JORDANNE

The answer is B

Tutorial note

The basic tax point for goods on sale or return is the earlier of the:

- expiry of the fixed time period for adopting the goods (provided that is within 12 months), or

- actual adoption of those goods.

The receipt of a payment for the goods is evidence that the customer has accepted the goods. Hence the customer has adopted the goods on 12 August.

An invoice is issued more than 14 days later, therefore the basic tax point is not overridden by the 14 day rule.

30 SCOTTY

The answer is D

Tutorial note

The receipt of a refundable deposit does not create a tax point.

The basic tax point for goods on sale or return is the earlier of the:

- expiry of the fixed time period for adopting the goods (provided that is within 12 months), or

- actual adoption of those goods.

Here the basic tax point is 10 June as the goods are adopted before the fixed time period expires.

An invoice is issued within 14 days of the basic tax point, therefore the 14 day rule applies and the tax point becomes 21 June.

Key answer tips

Information about this topic is included in the indirect tax reference material provided in the assessment, so you do not need to learn it.

However you need to be familiar with its location and content – why not look at it now?

31 KIM

The answer is B

Tutorial note

The basic tax point for services is when the service is performed. This is taken to be the date that all work has been completed except for invoicing.

In this case the work is completed on 3 December so this is the basic tax point.

The invoice is issued more than 14 days later so the 14 day rule does not apply.

Key answer tips

Information about this topic is included in the indirect tax reference material provided in the assessment, so you do not need to learn it.

However you need to be familiar with its location and content – why not look at it now?

32 BYRON

	True	False
If Byron invoices his customers on the last day of each month then that day will be the tax point.		✓
If Byron invoices his customers on the last day of each month then the tax point will be the 20th of each month.	✓	
Byron can invoice his customers annually in advance, setting out the schedule of payments for the year. If he does this his customers will be able to recover input tax for the year on receipt of that invoice, as the invoice date will be the tax point.		✓
Byron can invoice his customers annually in advance, setting out the schedule of payments for the year. If he does this there will be twelve separate monthly tax points.	✓	

Tutorial note

The leasing of the plant and machinery is a continuous service.

The basic tax point is the earlier of:

- *the date a VAT invoice is issued, or*

- *payment received.*

In this case the monthly direct debit is received before the VAT invoice is issued, so that fixes the tax point for each month.

However, when payments are received regularly a VAT invoice can be issued at the start of any period of up to one year (provided that more than one payment is due in the period) to cover all the payments due in that period.

For each payment the business should set out the following:

- *VAT-exclusive amount*

- *date on which the payment is due*

- *rate of VAT*

- *VAT payable*

In this case the business issuing the invoice does not have to pay all the VAT at the start of the year, but accounts for tax on the earlier of the:

- *payment date for each regular payment, or*

- *date payment received*

The customer can reclaim input tax at the same time.

Key answer tips

Information about this topic is included in the indirect tax reference material provided in the assessment, so you do not need to learn it.

However you need to be familiar with its location and content – why not look at it now?

33   DONNE

The answer is D

Tutorial note

When a business makes both taxable and exempt supplies, it can normally only recover input tax relating to making taxable supplies plus a proportion of the input tax relating to overheads.

However, if the remaining input tax does not exceed a de minimis figure then all of the input tax can be recovered.

VAT SCHEMES, DUE DATES, IRRECOVERABLE DEBT RELIEF

Key answer tips

The chief assessor has said in the past that the most common reasons for being not yet competent in questions on these areas were the use of and interaction between special schemes, and the effect of the cash accounting scheme on bad debt relief.

Candidates need to remember that if a business uses the cash accounting scheme then the usual procedure for bad debt relief is irrelevant.

Candidates must read tasks very carefully to establish whether:

(a)   there is a bad (irrecoverable) debt, and

(b)   the business can claim bad debt (irrecoverable debt) relief on the VAT return.

If the task sets out that the business uses cash accounting then it has no opportunity, or need, to claim this relief.

Another surprising area which has clearly been presenting problems is identifying the appropriate scheme for a business given specific information. Candidates should have enough time to access the right guidance in the indirect tax reference material to look up the rules to answer such questions.

34   WYE LTD

The answer is C

Tutorial note

When a business makes a VAT return it has one month and 7 days from the end of the VAT period to submit the return online.

35   RAVI

	True	False
VAT is normally payable at the same time that the return is due.	✓	
Paying VAT by direct debit gives the business an extra 5 bank working days from the normal payment date before payment is taken from the account.		✓
New businesses have a choice about whether they submit returns electronically or on paper.		✓
Quarterly VAT returns are all made up to 30 April, 31 July, 31 October and 31 January.		✓

Tutorial note

VAT payments are due at the same time as the return. Funds must clear HMRC bank account within 1 month and 7 days of the end of the VAT return period.

Direct debit payments are taken from the business bank account 3 bank working days from the normal payment date.

All new businesses have to use electronic returns. There is no choice.

There are three sets of quarterly return dates, not one. HMRC allocate businesses to one of the sets of dates to spread out the flow of returns submitted.

36   ANNUAL ACCOUNTING

(a)   The answer is C

(b)   The answer is B

(c)   The answer is B

(d)   The answer is B

Key answer tips

Note that this can be answered by looking in the indirect tax reference material provided in the assessment, so you do not need to learn it.

However you need to be familiar with its location and content – why not look at it now?

Tutorial note

The annual accounting scheme allows businesses to submit one VAT return each year. This is due two months after the year end. No seven day extension is allowed for electronic filing.

The scheme is not suitable for businesses which make zero-rated supplies. This is because such businesses can normally claim regular repayments of input tax as they have no output tax to pay over. If they choose annual accounting, they will only get one repayment per year.

VAT payments on account have to be made throughout the year. VAT is not just paid once a year with the return. These payments on account are based on last year's VAT liability. If a business has a reducing turnover of taxable supplies it will not benefit them to join the annual accounting scheme. This is because it will be making payments on account based on last year's higher VAT liability. If it used the normal accounting scheme it would be paying lower VAT payments based on the current year's liability.

37 ZED LTD

The answer is C

Payments on account are 10% of last year's liability of £7,290. Nine monthly payments are made at the end of months 4 to 12 in the accounting period.

38 TARAN

	True	False
Taxpayers must be up-to-date with their VAT returns before they are allowed to join the scheme.	✓	
Monthly payments on account are 10% of the previous year's VAT liability.	✓	
Monthly payments can be made using any method convenient to the taxpayer.		✓
Monthly payments are made 7 days after the end of the month.		✓
Monthly payments are made at the end of months 2 to 10 in the accounting period.		✓
The scheme allows businesses to budget for their VAT payments more easily.	✓	

Tutorial note

Payments must be made electronically with no extra 7 days allowed.

Payments are made at the end of months 4 to 12 during the accounting period not 2 to 10.

39 ARTHUR

Answers A and D are correct.

B is incorrect as traders can only join the scheme provided their annual taxable turnover does not exceed £1,350,000.

C is incorrect as VAT invoices still have to be sent to customers.

40 LAREDO

The answer is D

Tutorial note

With the cash accounting scheme, the tax point date is the date the payment is received.

41   CASH ACCOUNTING

	Will benefit	Will not benefit
A manufacturing business that sells all its output on credit to other businesses. Debtors take on average 45 days to pay. The business aims to pay creditors within 30 days of receiving purchase invoices.	✓	
A clothes shop based in a town centre which sells standard-rated supplies to members of the public for cash.		✓
A wholesaler who sells to other businesses on 40 days credit. In the last 12 months the business has suffered a steep rise in irrecoverable (bad) debts.	✓	
A business making solely zero-rated supplies to other businesses.		✓

Tutorial note

The cash accounting scheme allows businesses to pay output tax to HMRC when customers pay and to reclaim input tax when suppliers are paid. Output and input VAT totals are taken from the cash book.

The first business will benefit from the cash accounting scheme because they sell all their goods on credit. They will not have to pay over output VAT until their customers pay. Under the normal accounting scheme they would have to pay output VAT to HMRC before receiving cash from customers. There is a disadvantage because the business cannot reclaim input VAT until they pay for the goods but overall they should benefit.

The second business sells all its goods for cash, so adopting the cash accounting scheme makes no difference to the time they have to account for output VAT. However, with cash accounting the business cannot reclaim input VAT until they pay suppliers. This will delay the recovery of input VAT compared to the normal method.

The third business will benefit because with cash accounting there is no problem of irrecoverable (bad) debts from a VAT point of view. Using the normal accounting method a business must pay over VAT according to the normal tax point rules. This is usually before receiving cash from the customer. If the customer never pays, the business can claim back the output VAT paid but not until at least 6 months have passed. This is a cash flow disadvantage for the business which does not happen with cash accounting.

The fourth business makes zero-rated supplies so has no output tax to pay. However it can reclaim its input VAT, usually on a monthly basis. The business will not benefit from cash accounting because it would delay the time at which they could reclaim input tax.

42   FLAT RATE SCHEME

	Will benefit	Will not benefit
A business making solely zero-rated supplies to other businesses.		✓
A business with a lower than average (for their trade sector) level of input tax.	✓	
A business with a higher proportion of standard-rated supplies than other businesses in the same trade sector.	✓	

Tutorial note

When using the flat rate scheme, businesses calculate how much VAT to pay over to HMRC by using a fixed percentage of their VAT-inclusive total turnover (including exempt supplies).

If a business makes wholly zero-rated supplies their output VAT is £Nil and instead of having to pay VAT they can reclaim the input tax they have paid. With the flat rate scheme they would have to pay VAT instead of reclaiming it.

The flat rate percentage used by a business is fixed by reference to the average outputs less inputs for a typical business in that particular trade sector. If a business has lower than average inputs and hence input tax, they would benefit from using the flat rate scheme. Their overall VAT bill would be based on the higher trade sector proportion of inputs rather than their own lower figure.

The same logic would apply to the third business which has a higher proportion of standard-rated supplies. The trade percentage used in the flat rate scheme would be based on a lower average of taxable outputs and hence should produce less tax than using normal VAT accounting.

43   RAY

	True	False
A business can join the flat rate scheme provided their taxable turnover for the next 12 months is expected to be less than £230,000.		✓
VAT due to HMRC is calculated as a fixed percentage of VAT-inclusive taxable turnover.		✓
VAT invoices must still be issued.	✓	
A business can be in both the flat rate scheme and the annual accounting scheme at the same time.	✓	
The scheme cuts down on the time spent on VAT administration.	✓	
Businesses cannot pay less VAT under the flat rate scheme than the normal method of accounting for VAT.		✓

Tutorial note

A business can join the flat rate scheme provided their taxable turnover (excluding VAT) is less than £150,000. They have to leave the scheme when their total turnover exceeds £230,000 (including VAT and exempt supplies.)

The VAT calculation is based on VAT-inclusive TOTAL turnover, not just taxable turnover.

It is possible for a business to pay less VAT under the flat rate scheme than under the normal accounting scheme.

44 DERNBACH

The answer is C

VAT is calculated as 16.5% of £28,080 (£22,470 + £4,500 + £1,110) = £4,633.20.

The normal flat rate percentage must be replaced with 16.5% due to the business being a limited cost business.

45 SELDON

The answers are A and C

Answer A is wrong because the debt must simply have been written off. There is no time limit.

Answer C is wrong. There is no requirement that the customer should be formally insolvent, in administration or in liquidation.

Answers B and D are valid requirements.

Key answer tips

Information about this topic is included in the indirect tax reference material provided in the assessment , so you do not need to learn it.

However you need to be familiar with its location and content – why not look at it now?

DETAILED VAT RULES, SURCHARGES, PENALTIES AND CORRECTIONS

Key answer tips

The chief assessor has said in the past that the most common reasons for being not yet competent in tasks on these areas were: dealing with errors, the effect on VAT of deposits paid, and the charging of VAT on sales abroad.

Dealing with errors and omissions – common mistakes:

1   Failure to understand the error reporting threshold for separate notifications.

2   Belief that if a transaction was omitted from a previous return, it could be ignored – but omissions are errors and therefore action must be taken.

3   Not realising that a deliberate error is reportable, no matter what its value.

Too many candidates failed to understand the implications of deposits paid by a customer, and how this payment automatically creates a tax point for VAT and hence a reportable transaction.

Also, many candidates believed that a UK-registered business must charge VAT on standard-rated goods supplied to a VAT-registered business in the EU – instead of correctly treating such supplies as zero-rated.

46   LUIGI

The answer is D

Both standard-rated and zero-rated supplies are taxable supplies. If no exempt supplies are made then the business can recover all their input tax.

47   FORTE

The answer is B

Input VAT can be reclaimed on the staff entertaining and the van.

Total supplies on which VAT can be recovered £10,040 (£890 + £9,150).

This is a VAT-inclusive total so the VAT included is £1,673.33 (£10,040 × 20/120).

48   VINCENZO

Description	Net £	VAT £	Gross £	Reclaim input VAT?
Repairs to machinery	1,900.00	380.00	2,280.00	Yes
Delivery van	10,000.00	2,000.00	12,000.00	Yes
UK Customer entertaining	640.00	128.00	768.00	No
Overseas customer entertaining	310.00	62.00	372.00	Yes
Car (pool car with no private use)	8,400.00	1,680.00	10,080.00	Yes

Tutorial note

VAT cannot be recovered on entertaining, except for staff entertaining and entertaining overseas customers.

VAT cannot be recovered on the purchase of cars which have an element of private use.

Input VAT can be recovered on cars which are 100% used for the business, such as the pool car.

Key answer tips

Information about this topic is included in the indirect tax reference material provided in the assessment, so you do not need to learn it.

However you need to be familiar with its location and content – why not look at it now?

49   HOOCH LTD

The answer is C

	£
Output tax on scale charge (£295 × 20/120)	49.16
Input tax on petrol (£822.50 × 20/120)	(137.08)
Net Input tax recoverable	87.92

Tutorial note

When a business provides private fuel for an employee, a VAT scale charge depending on the CO_2 emission level of the car is added to outputs and output tax is increased.

Input tax on all the fuel paid for by the business can then be recovered.

Key answer tips

Information about this topic is included in the indirect tax reference material provided in the assessment, so you do not need to learn it.

However you need to be familiar with its location and content – why not look at it now?

50 RAFA AND CO

The answer is D

Options A, B and C mean that the business is only claiming business VAT so there is no need to account for a fuel scale charge.

Tutorial note

If a business does not want to pay a fuel scale charge then they can either:

(a) Reclaim only VAT on business fuel (detailed records of business and private mileage needs to be kept to prove the business mileage), or

(b) Not claim any VAT on fuel at all even for commercial vehicles. This has the advantage of being simple and is useful if mileage is low.

(c) Only use fuel for business purposes.

Key answer tips

Information about this topic is included in the indirect tax reference material provided in the assessment, so you do not need to learn it.

However you need to be familiar with its location and content – why not look at it now?

51 FINIAN

Item	Input tax recovered	Sale proceeds (excluding VAT)	Output VAT
		£	£.pp
Computer	Yes	400	80.00
Car	Yes	7,500	1,500.00
Van	Yes	6,100	1,220.00
Car	No	8,400	Nil

Tutorial note

Output tax must be charged on the sale of capital assets, except for cars where no input tax was recovered.

52   ALBERT

The answer is C

Input VAT can be recovered on half of the entertaining costs which relate to staff and on the van. No input VAT can be recovered on entertaining UK customers.

(£10,700 + (50% × £780)) × 1/6 = £1,848.33

53   VICTORIA LTD

The answer is D

Tutorial note

When a business provides private fuel for an employee, a VAT scale charge depending on the CO_2 emission level of the car is added to outputs and output tax is increased.

Input tax on all the fuel paid for by the business can then be recovered. In addition, VAT on all of the running costs may be recovered as the car is used partly for business purposes.

Key answer tips

Information about this topic is included in the indirect tax reference material provided in the assessment, so you do not need to learn it.

However you need to be familiar with its location and content – why not look at it now?

54   WELLES

The answer is A

Tutorial note

A business can reclaim the VAT according to the tax point of the purchase which is not necessarily the payment date. This is usually the date the goods/services are made available to the customer or when the invoice is issued (if that is within 14 days of delivery).

Key answer tips

Information about this topic is included in the indirect tax reference material provided in the assessment, so you do not need to learn it.

However you need to be familiar with its location and content – why not look at it now?

55   MELINDA

	Recover	Cannot recover
Purchases for resale	✓	
New laptop computer for Melinda's daughter		✓
New desk for the business office (Melinda has lost the VAT receipt)		✓
Motorcycle for business deliveries	✓	

Tutorial note

In order to claim back input VAT on goods or services, the trader must have a valid VAT invoice and the items must be for business use.

56   VAT PENALTIES

	True	False
Tax avoidance is a criminal offence and means using illegal means to reduce tax liability.		✓
A penalty can be charged if a trader fails to register at the correct time.	✓	
A registered trader who makes an error on a return leading to underpayment of tax will always be charged a penalty.		✓
If a registered trader does not submit a VAT return then HMRC can issue an assessment to collect VAT due.	✓	
A penalty can be charged if a trader fails to notify a significant change in their types of supply to HMRC within 30 days.	✓	

Tutorial note

The description given is of tax evasion. Tax avoidance means using lawful means to reduce your tax liability.

A penalty can be charged if a business does not register on time.

If an error is neither careless nor deliberate and the trader takes steps to correct it, then they may not be charged a penalty.

If a trader does not submit their VAT return then HMRC can issue an assessment showing the amount HMRC believes is due based on their best estimate.

Failure to notify HMRC of changes to details of VAT registration such as trading name or address, change of bank account details, change in main business activities or significant changes to types of supply, within 30 days can lead to a penalty.

57   VAT ERRORS

(a)

	Net error £	Turnover £	Include in next return	Separate disclosure
1	23,768	2,000,000		✓
2	7,150	85,400	✓	
3	35,980	4,567,090	✓	
4	61,600	10,000,000		✓

Tutorial note

When a trader discovers a VAT error they must inform HMRC. If the net error is less than a certain threshold and is not deliberate, it can be included on the next VAT return. If not, it must be disclosed separately on Form VAT 652 or in a letter.

The threshold operates as follows:

Net errors up to £10,000 can always be included on the next VAT return.

Net errors above £50,000 must always be separately disclosed.

Errors between these thresholds can be included on the next VAT return if they are no more than 1% of turnover (specifically the figure in Box 6 of the return).

(b)   Net error £41.86

	£
Output tax reduced by (£81 – £18)	63.00
Input tax reduced by	(21.14)
	41.86

This will reduce the VAT due.

Key answer tips

Information about this topic is included in the indirect tax reference material provided in the assessment, so you do not need to learn it.

However you need to be familiar with its location and content – why not look at it now?

58 DEFAULT SURCHARGE

(a)

	True	False
A default only occurs when a business pays its VAT late.		✓
A surcharge liability notice lasts for 6 months from the end of the period of default.		✓
Once a trader has received a surcharge liability notice, he must keep all his returns and payments up-to-date for the period of the surcharge notice, otherwise it will be extended.	✓	

Tutorial note

A default under the default surcharge scheme occurs when a trader files their VAT return late or pays its VAT late.

A surcharge liability notice lasts for 12 months not 6 months.

If the trader defaults again during the surcharge period they will have their surcharge period extended to 12 months after the end of the new period of default. If the default is a late payment they may also have to pay a penalty. Hence it is true to say that a business must 'keep out of trouble' for 12 months by paying VAT and submitting returns on time otherwise their surcharge period will be extended.

(b)   The answer is B

Tutorial note

When a business makes a VAT return they have one month and 7 days from the end of the VAT period to submit the return online.

The first time that a business submits a VAT return late, they are issued with a surcharge liability notice. This lasts 12 months and if the business pays late or submits their return late in the 12 month period it is extended. A late payment during the surcharge period attracts a surcharge penalty.

59 KEIKO LTD

The VAT due is £2,076.66

	£
Cash sales receipts	780
Receipts from customers	39,745
	40,525
Less: Cash paid to suppliers	(27,890)
Petty cash purchases	(175)
Net cash receipts	12,460
VAT at 20/120	2,076.66

Tutorial note

When a business uses cash accounting, the relevant figures for VAT are taken from cash receipts and payments rather than from invoiced amounts.

Cash receipts and payments made will be the VAT-inclusive amounts.

Note that the layout above is not intended to represent a VAT account or VAT return. It is just a working to calculate VAT due.

60 NOTICE

(a)   A business has received a surcharge liability notice from HMRC.

The notice would only have been issued if the business **had missed the due date for submitting its VAT return**.

The notice **puts the business in a surcharge period for 12 months**.

(b)   The answer is C

Tutorial note

Lack of funds to pay the tax is not a reasonable excuse, but the other reaons will be allowed as a reasonable excuse.

61   STANDARD PENALTIES

The answer is D

Tutorial note

Submission of late returns and late payment of VAT may result in a default surcharge, but not a standard penalty.

62   ERRORS AND OMISSIONS

Error/omissions		Action
Failing to register	C	HMRC can issue assessment to collect tax due and charge a penalty.
Failure to submit a return	B	HMRC can issue an assessment to collect tax due.
Making a careless or deliberate error	D	Trader must correct the error and HMRC can charge a penalty.
Making a non-careless error	A	Trader must correct the error.

63   PLACE OF SUPPLY

	Place of supply in UK	Place of supply in overseas country
Goods sold to unregistered customers	✓	
Goods sold to VAT registered customers	✓	
Services supplied to unregistered customers	✓	
Services supplied to VAT registered customers		✓

Key answer tips

Information about this topic is included in the indirect tax reference material provided in the assessment, so you do not need to learn it.

However you need to be familiar with its location and content – why not look at it now?

VAT CALCULATIONS AND RECONCILIATIONS

Key answer tips

The chief assessor has said in the past that the most common reason, by a significant margin, for being not yet competent in tasks on these areas is a problem in identifying errors that cause a discrepancy between the VAT account and the VAT return.

When the task sets out a failure to reconcile the VAT account and the VAT return, candidates need to take a step-by-step approach to the information provided. In most of these tasks there are two corrections to take into consideration. Candidates need to read the information given carefully and to practice this area more.

64   MURRAY LTD

The answer is B

The VAT due in the VAT control account is £2,485.40 too high.

This will occur if there are either too few debits or too many credits. Answer A would result in too many debits and hence a lower balance in the control account.

65   DARCY

The answer is B

The VAT control account balance shows £132.50 more due to HMRC than the VAT return calculations.

VAT on the bad debt recovered is £132.50 (£795 × 1/6). This would increase the output tax to be shown in the control account and would increase the balance of VAT due. This cannot explain the difference.

The credit note received from a supplier (a purchase credit note) also increases tax due to HMRC by £132.50 (£662.50 × 20%). This needs to be included in the VAT return calculations and will increase the VAT due to HMRC.

66   BINGLEY

The revised figure of VAT recoverable is £7,417.14

	£
Original VAT recoverable	2,947.64
Less: VAT due on fuel scale charges	(237.00)
Add: Bad debt (irrecoverable debt) relief (£4,239.00 × 1/6)	706.50
VAT recoverable on lorry purchase (£20,000 × 20%)	4,000.00
Revised figure of VAT recoverable	7,417.14

67   KYRA

The answer is D

	£
Value of supply	900.00
Less: Bulk buy discount (£900 × 2%)	(18.00)
	882.00
Less: Prompt payment discount (£882 × 5%)	(44.10)
Amount for calculation of VAT	837.90
VAT at 20%	167.58

Alternatively this could be calculated as (£900 × 98% × 95% × 20%)

Tutorial note
VAT must be accounted for on the amount that the customer actually pays.

68   LARISSA

(a)   The answer is B

	£
Value of supply	750.00
Less: Prompt payment discount (£750 × 3%)	(22.50)
Amount for calculation of VAT	727.50
VAT at 20%	145.50

Alternatively this could be calculated as (£750 × 97% × 20%)

(b)   The answer is D

	£
Discount (3% × £750.00)	22.50
VAT at 20%	4.50
	27.00

69   TRINA

The answer is B
VAT is £40.00 (£240.00 × 20/120)

Tutorial note
An offer to pay a customer's VAT is simply a form of discount. If the customer pays £240.00, this will be treated as the VAT-inclusive sale proceeds.

70 NASHEEN

The answer is D

	£ pp
AB Ltd (£562 × 20/120)	93.66
XY plc (£750 × 20%)	150.00
Total output tax	243.66

71 JULIE

The answer is B

Output VAT should be charged on the standard-rated sales and on the sale of plant.

Output VAT is £9,029.00 ((£40,145 + £5,000) × 20%).

72 COMFY SOFAS LTD

(£600 × 20/120) = £100

Tutorial note

An offer to pay a customer's VAT is simply a form of discount. If the customer pays £600.00, this will be treated as the VAT-inclusive sale proceeds.

73 FINN

	£
Value of supply	467.90
Less: Trade discount (£467.90 × 2%)	(9.36)
Amount for calculation of VAT	458.54
VAT at 20%	91.70

This can also be calculated as (£467.90 × 98% × 20%).

Tutorial note

VAT must be calculated after taking into account all possible discounts the customer could have.

The VAT on an invoice should be rounded down to the nearest penny (i.e. fractions of a penny are ignored).

74   AMANDA

	Increases balance payable to HMRC	Decreases balance payable to HMRC	No effect on balance payable to HMRC
VAT on purchases is understated		✓	
Bad debt relief claim omitted		✓	
Previous net over claim to be adjusted for on the next VAT return has been omitted	✓		
VAT on EU acquisition omitted			✓
Credit notes issued understated		✓	
VAT on sales overstated		✓	

Tutorial note

The VAT account per the VAT Guide is shown below.

If an entry is made on the debit side (left hand side) it reduces the amount payable to HMRC (unless it is credit notes received).

If an entry is made on the credit side (right hand side) it increases the amount payable to HMRC (unless it is credit notes issued).

VAT on EU acquisitions is entered on both sides of the VAT account and therefore has no effect on the balance payable to HMRC.

If credit notes issued are understated, the amendment will decrease the VAT payable.

VAT account

VAT deductible – input tax		VAT payable – output tax	
	£ p		£ p
VAT suffered on purchases	X	VAT charged on sales	X
VAT suffered on imports	X		
VAT allowable on acquisitions from EU	X	VAT due on acquisitions from EU	X
Adjustments of previous errors (if within error limit)			
Net input tax adjustment	X	Net output tax adjustment	X
Bad debt (irrecoverable debt) relief	X		
Less: VAT on credit notes received	(X)	Less: VAT on credit notes allowed to customers	(X)
Total tax deductible	X	Total tax payable	X
		Total tax deductible	(X)
		Payable to HMRC	X

75   ASHWIN

The answer is B

A VAT payment should be debited to the VAT account but it has been credited in error. This means that the account is showing too many credits.

The credit side is £14,271.60 (2 × £7,135.80) too high and the uncorrected balance must be £19,961.82 (£5,690.22 + £14,271.60).

76   REHMAN

The answer is C

The VAT account is showing a debit balance that is too high by £719.50 indicating that too many debits have been posted.

VAT on sales invoices should be credited to the VAT account so if posted on the wrong side (i.e. debit), this would explain the difference.

The amount posted on the wrong side is half of the error in the balance (i.e. half of £719.50 which is £359.75).

77   ANGELO

The correct answer is C

The nature of the sales made by Angelo would not affect purchase invoices raised by his suppliers.

Option A can explain the shortfall in VAT as this could be a simple error in calculation.

If a trader offers a discount (option B) then the VAT is calculated on the fully discounted amount and not the purchase price of the goods.

If some of the supplies were zero-rated (option D) then the VAT would only be charged on the taxable supplies and not the total amount of supplies.

78   ALYSSA

The price of £487 is the price paid by the customer and hence includes VAT.

The VAT is therefore = (£487 × 20/120) = £81.16

Tutorial note

When a business offers to pay a customer's VAT this is just another form of discount.

The amount paid by the customer will be the VAT-inclusive amount. The VAT to be accounted for by the business is therefore 20/120 of the amount paid.

79   HOLLY

The final figure of output tax will be £3,898.40

	£
Original output VAT figure	3,556.40
Less: VAT overstated (£297.55 – £279.55)	(18.00)
	3,538.40
Add: VAT understated (£840.00 – £480.00)	360.00
Revised output VAT figure	3,898.40

PREPARING SPECIFIC FIGURES FOR THE VAT RETURN

Key answer tips

The chief assessor has said in the past that it is clear that weaker candidates make more than one error in this task, even though the adjustments required to the figures from the accounting extracts are never particularly difficult.

A well-prepared candidate should be able to work out where to make the changes, but too many simply use the base values from the accounting extracts and ignore, it seems, the additional information about adjustments.

Candidates need to read the information about adjustments carefully. For example, if it states that 'bad debt relief of £100 is to be claimed', the figure of £100 should be added to Box 4, not 20% of £100.

80   PATEL

Irrecoverable (bad) debt relief can be claimed on the debts of £4,200 and £6,552 only.

The amount claimed = (£4,200 + £6,552) × 20/120 = £1,792.

No relief can be claimed on the debts of £7,000 and £2,500 as the end of the quarter (i.e. 30 September X1) is not 6 months since the later of the:

- date of supply, or
- date payment was due.

Tutorial note

Unless a business uses a special accounting scheme, output tax is due at the normal tax point date. This will usually be before the customer has paid.

If the customer never pays, the business can claim back the output VAT paid over on the sale provided the following conditions are met:

(i)   Output VAT on the original invoice has been paid to HMRC.

(ii)   Six months have elapsed since the later of the date of supply or the date payment was due.

(iii)   The debt has been written off as irrecoverable in the financial accounting records.

The VAT on the irrecoverable (bad) debt is included in Box 4 on the VAT return.

Key answer tips

Information about this topic is included in the indirect tax reference material provided in the assessment, so you do not need to learn it.

However you need to be familiar with its location and content – why not look at it now?

81   JASPER

		£
VAT due in the period on **acquisitions** from other **EU Member States**	**Box 2**	5,480.00
VAT reclaimed in the period on **purchases** and other inputs, including acquisitions from the EU	**Box 4**	23,960.00
Total value of purchases and all other inputs excluding any VAT. **Include your box 9 figure**	**Box 7**	119,800
Total value of all **acquisitions** of goods and related costs, excluding any VAT, from other **EU Member States**	**Box 9**	27,400

Workings

Box 2	VAT on acquisitions from other EU countries	
	(20% × £27,400)	£5,480.00
Box 4	VAT reclaimed	
	20% × (£54,800 + £27,400 + £37,600)	£23,960.00
Box 7	Total purchases	
	(£54,800 + £27,400 + £37,600)	£119,800
Box 9	Purchases from other EU countries	£27,400

Tutorial note

Purchases (acquisitions) from EU businesses are dealt with as follows:

- *The business must account for both output and input VAT.*
- *The VAT on these purchases is included in Box 2 and then again as part of the input VAT in Box 4.*

The net value of the purchases is included in the inputs in Box 7 and again in Box 9.

Key answer tips

Information about this topic is included in the indirect tax reference material provided in the assessment, so you do not need to learn it.

However you need to be familiar with its location and content – why not look at it now?

82 MISTRY

(a) Calculate the figure for Box 2 of the VAT return – VAT due on acquisitions from other EU member states.

£3,000.00

(b) Calculate the figure for Box 1 of the VAT return – VAT due on sales and other outputs.

£132,200.00

(c) Calculate the figure for box 4 of the VAT return – VAT reclaimed on purchases and other inputs, including acquisitions from the EU.

£65,200.00

Workings

(a) (£15,000.00 × 20%) = £3,000.00

(b) (£134,000.00 – £1,800.00) = £132,200.00

(c) (£62,200 + £3,000) = £65,200.00

Key answer tips

Information about this topic is included in the indirect tax reference material provided in the assessment, so you do not need to learn it.

However you need to be familiar with its location and content – why not look at it now?

83   FLETCH

(a)   Calculate the figure for Box 1 of the VAT return – VAT due on sales and other outputs.

21,623.70

(b)   Calculate the figure for box 4 of the VAT return – VAT reclaimed on purchases and other inputs, including acquisitions from the EU.

37,186.68

(c)   Calculate the figure for Box 7 of the VAT return – value of purchases and all other inputs, excluding any VAT. Whole pounds only.

235,080

Workings

(a)   (£20,265.67 + £1,358.03) = £21,623.70

(b)   (£43,308.08 – (£30,607 × 20%) irrecoverable VAT on company car) = £37,186.68

(c)   Box 7 includes all purchases (including zero rated purchases, the company car and the van) but excluding VAT.

Tutorial note

Note that there is no adjustment made for the irrecoverable VAT on the company car to calculate the purchases figure for Box 7. The irrecoverable VAT on the car will be added to purchases for the purposes of compiling the statement of profit or loss, but is not included in the VAT return in Box 7.

Key answer tips

Information about this topic is included in the indirect tax reference material provided in the assessment, so you do not need to learn it.

However you need to be familiar with its location and content – why not look at it now.

84 HARDACRE

(a)   Calculate the figure to be reclaimed as irrecoverable debt relief on the VAT return.

£337.82

(b)   Calculate the figure for Box 1 of the VAT return – VAT due on sales and other outputs.

£101,336.00

(c)   Calculate the figure for box 4 of the VAT return – VAT reclaimed on purchases and other inputs, including acquisitions from the EC.

£50,074.00

Workings

(a)   (£1,689.10 × 20%) = £337.82

(b)   (£92,156.00 + £9,180) = £101,336.00

(c)   (£49,736.18 + £337.82 irrecoverable (bad) debt relief) = £50,074.00

Tutorial note

Export sales are zero-rated. The term exports means sales outside the EU.

Unless a business uses a special accounting scheme, output tax is due at the normal tax point date. This will usually be before the customer has paid. If the customer never pays, the business can claim back the output VAT paid over on the sale provided the following conditions are met:

(i)   Output VAT on the original invoice has been paid to HMRC.

(ii)   Six months have elapsed since the later of the date of supply or the date payment was due.

(iii)   The debt has been written off as irrecoverable in the financial accounting records.

The VAT on the irrecoverable (bad) debt is included in Box 4 on the VAT return.

Key answer tips

Information about this topic is included in the indirect tax reference material provided in the assessment, so you do not need to learn it.

However you need to be familiar with its location and content – why not look at it now.

85   SPRINGER

(a)   Calculate the figure for irrecoverable (bad) debt relief.

£416.11

(b)   Calculate the figure for Box 3 of the VAT return – total VAT due.

11,009.00

(c)   Calculate the figure for Box 4 of the VAT return – VAT reclaimed on purchases and other inputs, including acquisitions from the EC.

7,650.11

Workings

		£.pp
(a)	Irrecoverable (bad) debt relief £2,496.66 × 20/120 (or 1/6)	416.11
		———
(b)	Sales invoices issued	67,800
	Cash sales receipts	234
	Sales credit notes	(1,980)
		———
		66,054
		———
	VAT at 20/120	11,009.00
		———
(c)	Purchase invoices	45,350
	Petty cash purchases	154
	Purchase debit notes	(2,100)
		———
		43,404
		———
	VAT at 20/120	7,234.00
	Add: Irrecoverable (bad) debt relief	416.11
		———
		7,650.11
		———

Tutorial note

If a buyer returns goods to their supplier they have three options:

1   Return their original invoice and receive a replacement invoice with the correct amount of VAT.

2   Obtain a credit note from the supplier.

3   Issue a debit note to their supplier.

A purchase credit or debit note reduces input VAT that the business can reclaim.

From the point of view of the supplier a debit note received or a sales credit note issued will reduce output VAT.

86   JACOB

(a)   Calculate the figure for Box 1 of the VAT return – VAT due in the period on sales and other outputs.

> 96,834.80

(b)   Calculate the figure for Box 4 of the VAT return – VAT reclaimed on purchases and other inputs, including acquisitions from the EU.

> 40,538.80

(c)   Calculate the figure for Box 6 of the VAT return – total value of sales and other outputs excluding any VAT. Whole pounds only.

> 519,574

Workings

		£.pp
(a)	On sales – per VAT account	94,600.00
	On sales returns – per VAT account	(800.00)
	VAT on imports of services (£15,174 × 20%)	3,034.80
		96,834.80
(b)	On purchases – per VAT account	37,504.00
	VAT on imports of services	3,034.80
		40,538.80
(c)	Sales per sales account	473,000
	Sales returns – per sales account	(4,000)
	Imports of services	15,174
	Despatches to EU	35,400
		519,574

Tutorial note

Services supplied to businesses within the EU follow the 'reverse charge' principle. The acquiring business is treated as if it had supplied the services to itself and VAT will be accounted for at the rate applicable to that type of supply in the customer's home country.

Output tax must be paid by the acquiring business and included in Box 1 of the return. It can then be recovered by including it in Box 4 of the return.

The net value of the supply must then be included in Box 6 (sales) and Box 7 (purchases).

COMPLETING AND SUBMITTING A VAT RETURN ACCURATELY

Key answer tips

The chief assessor has said in the past that the most common reason for being not yet competent in questions on this area is lack of practice and failing to complete the boxes accurately, making sure for instance that whole pounds only are used in Boxes 6 to 9, as clearly indicated on the return.

87   DAVIES LTD

VAT return to 31 May 20X2

		£
VAT due in the period on **sales** and other outputs	Box 1	88,164.00
VAT due in the period on **acquisitions** from other **EU Member States**	Box 2	0.00
Total VAT due (**the sum of boxes 1 and 2**)	Box 3	88,164.00
VAT reclaimed in the period on **purchases** and other inputs, including acquisitions from the EU	Box 4	34,493.05
Net VAT to be paid to HM Revenue & Customs or reclaimed (**Difference between boxes 3 and 4**)	Box 5	53,670.95
Total value of **sales** and all other outputs excluding any VAT. **Include your box 8 figure**	Box 6	600,160
Total value of purchases and all other inputs excluding any VAT. **Include your box 9 figure**	Box 7	199,720
Total value of all **supplies** of goods and related costs, excluding any VAT, to other **EU Member States**	Box 8	107,240
Total value of all **acquisitions** of goods and related costs, excluding any VAT, from other **EU Member States**	Box 9	0

Workings

	£.pp
Box 1 – Output tax	
March	24,200.00
April	35,804.00
May	28,160.00
	88,164.00
Box 4 – Input tax	
March	13,840.00
April	12,636.00
May	13,468.00
Less: Input tax over claim	(5,450.95)
	34,493.05

	£
Box 6 – Total outputs	
UK sales (£121,000 + £179,020 + £140,800)	440,820
EU sales (£30,300 + £41,160 + £35,780)	107,240
Exports (£17,000 + £14,900 + £20,200)	52,100
	600,160
Box 7 – Total inputs	
March	69,200
April	63,180
May	67,340
	199,720

Tutorial note

1   *Purchases and sales figures extracted from ledgers will always be net of VAT.*

2   *Export sales are dealt with as follows:*

Sales to registered businesses in the EU are zero-rated so there is no output VAT to include in Box 1. The sales are part of the total outputs included in Box 6 and are also entered in Box 8.

Sales to non-registered customers in the EU are treated just like normal UK sales and are not included in Box 8.

Sales to customers outside the EU are zero-rated and they only appear on the VAT return as part of the outputs in Box 6.

3   When a trader discovers a VAT error they must inform HMRC. If the net error is less than a certain threshold and is not deliberate it can be included on the next VAT return. If not, it must be disclosed separately on Form VAT 652 or in a letter.

The threshold operates as follows:

Net errors up to £10,000 can always be included on the next VAT return.
Net errors above £50,000 must always be separately disclosed.

Errors between these thresholds can be included on the next VAT return if they are no more than 1% of turnover (specifically the figure in Box 6 of the return).

Key answer tips

Information about this topic is included in the indirect tax reference material provided in the assessment, so you do not need to learn it.

However you need to be familiar with its location and content – why not look at it now?

88   TROTT

VAT return to 31 March 20X5

		£
VAT due in the period on **sales** and other outputs	**Box 1**	1,452.00
VAT due in the period on **acquisitions** from other **EC Member States**	**Box 2**	0.00
Total VAT due (**the sum of boxes 1 and 2**)	**Box 3**	1,452.00
VAT reclaimed in the period on **purchases** and other inputs, including acquisitions from the EC	**Box 4**	824.16
Net VAT to be paid to HM Revenue & Customs or reclaimed (**Difference between boxes 3 and 4**)	**Box 5**	627.84
Total value of **sales** and all other outputs excluding any VAT. **Include your box 8 figure**	**Box 6**	7,260
Total value of purchases and all other inputs excluding any VAT. **Include your box 9 figure**	**Box 7**	10,525
Total value of all **supplies** of goods and related costs, excluding any VAT, to other **EC Member States**	**Box 8**	0
Total value of all **acquisitions** of goods and related costs, excluding any VAT, from other **EC Member States**	**Box 9**	0

Workings

£.pp

Box 1 – Output tax

Sales day book	1,470.00
Cash receipts book	52.00
	1,522.00
Less: Sales credit note day book	(70.00)
	1,452.00

Box 4 – Input tax

Purchase day book	722.00
Cash payments book	30.00
Petty cash book	33.00
Irrecoverable (bad) debt relief (£235 × 20/120)	39.16
	824.16

£

Box 6 – Total outputs

Sales day book	7,350
Cash receipts book	260
	7,610
Less: Sales credit note day book	(350)
	7,260

Box 7 – Total inputs

Purchase day book (£2,160 + £1,450)	3,610
Cash payments book	150
Petty cash book	165
Car (excluding VAT) (£7,920 × 100/120)	6,600
	10,525

Tutorial note

1   Unless a business uses a special accounting scheme, output tax is due at the normal tax point date. This will usually be before the customer has paid. If the customer never pays, the business can claim back the output VAT paid over on the sale provided the following conditions are met:

(i)   Output VAT on the original invoice has been paid to HMRC.

(ii)   Six months have elapsed since the later of the date of supply or the date payment was due.

(iii)   The debt has been written off as irrecoverable in the financial accounting records.

The VAT on the irrecoverable (bad) debt is included in Box 4.

> 2   *When you are given figures from cash receipt or payment books you are not interested in the amounts received from debtors or paid to creditors, unless the business uses the cash accounting scheme.*
>
> *The information we need from cash books (including petty cash books) is the amount of any cash purchases and expenses, and any cash sales, plus the related VAT.*
>
> *The VAT on credit sales and purchases is taken from the daybooks.*
>
> *Sales credit notes are deducted from sales for Box 6 and the VAT on sales credit notes is deducted from the output tax in Box 1.*
>
> 3   *VAT on the car purchase cannot be reclaimed so the input VAT must not be included in the Box 4 figure. However, the VAT-exclusive amount is included in Box 7.*

89   BARTLET LTD

VAT return for the quarter ended 30 September 20X2

		£
VAT due in the period on **sales** and other outputs	**Box 1**	4,340.00
VAT due in the period on **acquisitions** from other **EU Member States**	**Box 2**	572.00
Total VAT due (**the sum of boxes 1 and 2**)	**Box 3**	4,912.00
VAT reclaimed in the period on **purchases** and other inputs, including acquisitions from the EU	**Box 4**	4,100.00
Net VAT to be paid to HM Revenue & Customs or reclaimed (**Difference between boxes 3 and 4**)	**Box 5**	812.00
Total value of **sales** and all other outputs excluding any VAT. **Include your box 8 figure**	**Box 6**	45,675
Total value of purchases and all other inputs excluding any VAT. **Include your box 9 figure**	**Box 7**	20,500
Total value of all **supplies** of goods and related costs, excluding any VAT, to other **EU Member States**	**Box 8**	5,105
Total value of all **acquisitions** of goods and related costs, excluding any VAT, from other **EU Member States**	**Box 9**	2,860

Workings

	£.pp
Box 1 – Output tax	
On UK standard-rated sales	4,100.00
On sales to EU non-registered customers	240.00
	4,340.00
Box 4 – Input tax	
On UK purchases and expenses	3,400.00
Purchases from EU businesses	572.00
Petty cash book	128.00
	4,100.00

	£
Box 6 – Total outputs	
UK standard-rated sales	20,500
UK zero-rated sales	13,470
UK exempt sales	1,650
Sales to VAT-registered EU customers	5,105
Sales to non VAT-registered EU customers	1,200
Exports outside the EU	3,750
	45,675
Box 7 – Total inputs	
UK purchases and expenses	17,000
Purchases from EU businesses	2,860
Petty cash purchases and expenses	640
	20,500

Tutorial note

1   *Export sales are dealt with as follows:*

Sales to registered businesses in the EU are zero-rated so there is no output VAT to include in Box 1. The sales are part of the total outputs included in Box 6 and are also entered in Box 8.

Sales to non VAT-registered customers in the EU are treated just like normal UK sales and are not included in Box 8.

Sales to customers outside the EU are zero-rated and they only appear on the VAT return as part of the outputs in Box 6.

> 2   *Purchases (acquisitions) from EU businesses are dealt with as follows:*
>
> *The business must account for both output and input VAT.*
>
> *The VAT on these purchases is included in Box 2 and then again as part of the input VAT in Box 4.*
>
> *The net value of the purchases is included in the inputs in Box 7 and again in Box 9.*
>
> 3   *Exempt sales must be included as part of the outputs in Box 6.*
>
> 4   *Wages are outside the scope of VAT and are not included on the VAT return.*

Key answer tips

Information about accounting for overseas sales and purchases is included in the indirect tax reference material provided in the assessment, so you do not need to learn it.

However you need to be familiar with its location and content – why not look at it now?

90   O'BRIEN

VAT return for the quarter ended 30 June 20X0

		£
VAT due in the period on **sales** and other outputs	**Box 1**	149,386.92
VAT due in the period on **acquisitions** from other **EU Member States**	**Box 2**	6,337.72
Total VAT due (**the sum of boxes 1 and 2**)	**Box 3**	155,724.64
VAT reclaimed in the period on **purchases** and other inputs, including acquisitions from the EU	**Box 4**	114,065.89
Net VAT to be paid to HM Revenue & Customs or reclaimed (**Difference between boxes 3 and 4**)	**Box 5**	41,658.75
Total value of **sales** and all other outputs excluding any VAT. **Include your box 8 figure**	**Box 6**	828,495
Total value of purchases and all other inputs excluding any VAT. **Include your box 9 figure**	**Box 7**	570,329
Total value of all **supplies** of goods and related costs, excluding any VAT, to other **EU Member States**	**Box 8**	0
Total value of all **acquisitions** of goods and related costs, excluding any VAT, from other **EU Member States**	**Box 9**	31,689

Workings

	£.pp
Box 1 – Output tax	
UK sales	137,911.14
UK cash sales	6,535.78
VAT on imports of services (£24,700 × 20%)	4,940.00
	149,386.92
Box 4 – Input tax	
UK purchases	102,788.17
VAT on EU acquisitions	6,337.72
VAT on imports of services (£24,700 × 20%)	4,940.00
	114,065.89
Box 6 – Sales per sales account	803,795
Imports of services	24,700
	828,495
Box 7 – Purchases	545,629
Imports of services	24,700
	570,329

Tutorial note

1   *Purchases (acquisitions) from EU businesses are dealt with as follows:*

The business must account for both output and input VAT.

The VAT on these purchases is included in Box 2 and then again as part of the input VAT in Box 4.

The net value of the purchases is included in the inputs in Box 7 and again in Box 9.

2   *Services supplied to businesses within the EU follow the 'reverse charge' principle. The acquiring business is treated as if it had supplied the services to itself and VAT will be accounted for at the rate applicable to that type of supply in the customer's home country.*

Output tax must be paid by the acquiring business and included in Box 1 of the return. It can then be recovered by including it in Box 4 of the return.

The net value of the supply must then be included in Box 6 (sales) and Box 7 (purchases).

3   *Purchases and sales figures extracted from ledgers will always be net of VAT.*

Key answer tips

Information about these topics is included in the indirect tax reference material provided in the assessment, so you do not need to learn it.

However you need to be familiar with its location and content – why not look at it now?

91 STEWART LTD (1)

VAT return to 31 October 20X5

		£
VAT due in the period on **sales** and other outputs	**Box 1**	28,376.40
VAT due in the period on **acquisitions** from other **EC Member States**	**Box 2**	2,918.60
Total VAT due (**the sum of boxes 1 and 2**)	**Box 3**	31,295.00
VAT reclaimed in the period on **purchases** and other inputs, including acquisitions from the EC	**Box 4**	22,227.80
Net VAT to be paid to HM Revenue & Customs or reclaimed (**Difference between boxes 3 and 4**)	**Box 5**	9,067.20
Total value of **sales** and all other outputs excluding any VAT. **Include your box 8 figure**	**Box 6**	141,882
Total value of purchases and all other inputs excluding any VAT. **Include your box 9 figure**	**Box 7**	111,139
Total value of all **supplies** of goods and related costs, excluding any VAT, to other **EC Member States**	**Box 8**	0
Total value of all **acquisitions** of goods and related costs, excluding any VAT, from other **EC Member States**	**Box 9**	14,593

Workings

	£.pp
Box 1 – Output tax	
Per the ledger	28,376.40
Box 2 – VAT due on acquisitions from other EC states	
Purchases from EC businesses (£14,593 × 20%)	2,918.60

	£.pp
Box 4 – Input tax	
On UK purchases and expenses	15,309.20
Purchases from EC businesses	2,918.60
VAT on purchase of lorry	4,000.00
	22,227.80
Box 6 – Total outputs	
UK sales	145,450
Less: Credit notes	(3,568)
	141,882
Box 7 – Total inputs	
UK purchases	59,678
Expenses	19,437
Purchases from EC businesses	14,593
Purchase of lorry	20,000
Less: Purchase credit notes	(2,569)
	111,139

Tutorial note

1   *Purchases and sales figures extracted from ledgers will always be net of VAT.*

2   *Purchases (acquisitions) from EC businesses are dealt with as follows:*

   The business must account for both output and input VAT.

   The VAT on these purchases is included in Box 2 and then again as part of the input VAT in Box 4.

   The net value of the purchases is included in the inputs in Box 7 and again in Box 9.

3   *Wages are outside the scope of VAT and are not included on the VAT return.*

Key answer tips

Information about EC sales and purchases and VAT on motor expenses, is included in the indirect tax reference material provided in the assessment, so you do not need to learn it.

However you need to be familiar with its location and content – why not look at it now?

COMMUNICATING VAT INFORMATION

Key answer tips

The chief assessor has said in the past that the most common reason for being not yet competent in questions on this area is not reading the task properly and then failing to provide the correct information to others in the organisation.

For example, where the business's input tax exceeds the output tax for the VAT period there will be a refund due to the business from HMRC, but some candidates failed to appreciate this. They identified the correct value to enter on the e-mail but advised the finance representative to make a payment when a refund is due, or vice versa.

For such a straightforward task, much more care is needed.

92   STEWART LTD (2)

Email	
To:	Financial accountant
From:	Accounting technician
Date:	17 November 20X5
Subject:	VAT return and capital expenditure

Please be advised that I have just completed the VAT return for the quarter ended **31 October 20X5**.

The amount of VAT **payable** will be £13,067.20.

The return must be with HMRC on or before **7 December 20X5**.

The VAT will be **paid electronically by 7 December 20X5**.

I **have not** included the invoice for capital expenditure. VAT of **£4,000.00 cannot** be reclaimed on this expenditure in the current quarter.

Kind regards

Working

VAT due is £13,067.20 (£9,067.20 per the previous answer plus £4,000 input VAT that cannot be claimed).

Tutorial note

It is important that you can demonstrate that you have professional ethics and can correctly deal with pressure to allow irrecoverable VAT or other inappropriate amounts to appear in the VAT return.

93   DHONI LTD

Email
To: Financial Accountant
From: Accounting technician
Date: 17 January 20X3
Subject: VAT error

An error occurred in the VAT return for the previous quarter. Output VAT of £4,672.90 was **understated.** This resulted in VAT being **underpaid.**

This error **was included on the VAT return to 31 December.**

Kind regards

Tutorial note

When a trader discovers a VAT error they must inform HMRC.

If the net error is less than a certain threshold and is not deliberate it can be included on the next VAT return. If not, it must be disclosed separately on Form VAT 652 or in a letter.

The threshold operates as follows:

- *Net errors up to £10,000 can always be included on the next VAT return.*

- *Net errors above £50,000 must always be separately disclosed.*

Errors between these thresholds can be included on the next VAT return if they are no more than 1% of turnover (specifically the figure in Box 6 of the return).

Key answer tips

Information about this topic is included in the indirect tax reference material provided in the assessment, so you do not need to learn it.

However you need to be familiar with its location and content – why not look at it now?

94   BELL

Email
To: Andrew Bell
From: Accounting technician
Date: 17 April 20X5
Subject: Irrecoverable (bad) debt relief
Thank you for advising me about the debt you wrote off. I have included relief for this in the VAT return for the quarter ended **31 March 20X5**.
Relief can be claimed because the debt was due for payment more than **6 months** ago.
The **output** tax paid on the original invoice can be reclaimed by including the amount in **Box 4.** The amount of irrecoverable (bad) debt relief is **£1,077.83**.
Kind regards

Key answer tips

Information about this topic is included in the indirect tax reference material provided in the assessment, so you do not need to learn it.

However you need to be familiar with its location and content – why not look at it now?

95   SEABORN LTD

Email
To: Financial Accountant
From: Accounting Technician
Date: 5 September 20X6
Subject: Filing VAT returns
VAT returns must be submitted **quarterly** unless you are a net repayment trader when returns can be made **monthly**.
Returns must be filed within **1 month** after the end of the VAT period with an extension of **7 days** where returns are filed online.
You **must file online.**
Kind regards

Key answer tips

Information about this topic is included in the indirect tax reference material provided in the assessment, so you do not need to learn it.

However you need to be familiar with its location and content – why not look at it now?

96   MILES LTD

Email
To: All Sales and Sales Invoicing Staff
From: Accounts Assistant
Date: 14 July 20X2
Subject: Change in VAT treatment

As you know the company's main product has been reclassified from one that is **zero-rated** to one that is **standard-rated**.

All sales invoices **with a tax point on or after 1 September** must have the standard rate of VAT applied.

As we have decided to keep our VAT-inclusive prices the same, the price of goods to our customers will **stay the same** and our profits will **decrease**.

Kind regards

Key answer tips

Information about this topic is included in the indirect tax reference material provided in the assessment, so you do not need to learn it.

97   ELSIE

The answer is C

It is important that you identify when a query about VAT is beyond your current expertise and hence refer it to a line manager.

Section 3

MOCK ASSESSMENT QUESTIONS

TASK 1   **(Total 6 marks)**

(a)   Joe starts his business on 1 June 20X1.

       He has taxable supplies of £8,600 per month.   **(3 marks)**

       (i)   When does he need to notify HMRC?   Day _____Month_____Year_____

       (ii)   What date will he be registered from?   Day _____Month_____Year_____

       (iii)   Can he register voluntarily before this date?   YES/NO

(b)   Are the following statements true or false?   **(3 marks)**

       Tick the correct box for each statement.

	True	False
A business has an expected turnover for the next 12 months of £87,000 but it sells goods that are zero-rated so it cannot register for VAT.		
VAT records should normally be kept for 4 years.		
Business records that should be kept include order books.		
If you want to find out information about registering for VAT the first thing you should do is write to HMRC for information.		
It is important for an AAT member to keep up-to-date to ensure client confidentiality.		
If a business fails to register for VAT then HMRC will collect any VAT due but will not issue a penalty.		

TASK 2   **(Total 9 marks)**

(a)   A business makes a purchase of materials on sale or return. The goods are delivered on 12 May 20X2 and must be accepted or returned by 31 August 20X2. The business decides to accept the goods on 20 July 20X2 and pays for them on 30 July 20X2. The invoice was issued on 10 August 20X2.

       What is the actual tax point for this purchase?   **(1 mark)**

       A   12 May 20X2

       B   20 July 20X2

       C   30 July 20X2

       D   12 August 20X2

(b)   If you send a sales credit note to a customer for £40 plus standard rate VAT, what effect does this have on the amount of VAT payable to HMRC by your business?   **(2 marks)**

A   The amount payable will decrease by £40

B   The amount payable will increase by £40

C   The amount payable will decrease by £8

D   The amount payable will increase by £8

(c)   A business supplies goods that are a mixture of standard-rated and exempt.   **(2 marks)**

Which one of the following statements is true?

A   All of the input VAT can be reclaimed

B   None of the input VAT can be reclaimed

C   All of the input VAT can be reclaimed provided certain de minimis conditions are met

D   Only the input VAT on goods and services purchased for use in making standard-rated supplies can ever be reclaimed

(d)   Look at the following list of items.   **(4 marks)**

Select by entering the appropriate number whether the items:

1   Should only be shown on a normal detailed VAT invoice; or

2   Should be shown on both a normal detailed VAT invoice and on a simplified invoice or

3   Should not be shown on either form of invoice.

	Item	Number (1, 2, or 3)
A	Identifying number	
B	Delivery date	
C	Total amount of VAT payable	
D	Customer's registration number	

TASK 3   **(Total 5 marks)**

(a)   Which of the following is an advantage of the annual accounting scheme?   **(1 mark)**

A   It is good for businesses that are experiencing a decrease in turnover compared to previous years

B   It is beneficial for businesses that have a repayment due to them rather than having to make a payment of VAT

C   It reduces the amount of administration work to be completed

(b) Jasper Enterprises uses the annual accounting scheme. Their annual period ends on 31 May. The VAT liability for the year ended 31 May 20X1 is £6,980 and for the year ended 31 May 20X2 is £7,211.

(i) What monthly payments on account should the business make for the year ended 31 May 20X2? **(1 mark)**

[   ]

(ii) What is the balancing payment for the year ended 31 May 20X2? **(1 mark)**

[   ]

(c) Are the following statements true or false? **(2 marks)**

Tick the correct box for each statement.

	True	False
Irrecoverable (bad) debt relief is available for all debts written off by a business provided the debt is over 3 months old.		
A business has prepared its VAT return for the quarter ended 31 March 20X2; it must pay by electronic transfer by 30 April 20X2.		

TASK 4 (Total 9 marks)

(a) State whether input VAT can be reclaimed on each of the purchases below. All purchases are made by a business for business purposes. The car is used by the managing director for both business and private mileage. **(4 marks)**

Item	Net £	VAT £	Gross £	Reclaim?
Motor car	2,500.00	500.00	3,000.00	
Stationery	25.00	5.00	30.00	
Fixtures and fittings	1,212.00	242.40	1,454.40	
Staff entertaining	250.00	50.00	300.00	

(b) For each of the following businesses, indicate whether they can correct their (non-deliberate) errors on their next VAT return or whether they are required to make separate disclosure (tick the appropriate box). **(3 marks)**

	On next return	Separate disclosure
(i) A business with a net error of £15,552 and a turnover of £2,800,000.		
(ii) A business with a net error of £8,032 and a turnover of £58,000.		
(iii) A business with a net error of £12,156 and a turnover of £810,000.		

(c)   Are the following statements true or false?   **(2 marks)**

Tick the correct box for each statement.

	True	False
A business that always pays its VAT on time, but for the first time submits its VAT return late, will not be issued with a surcharge liability notice.		
If a business makes a careless error it must notify HMRC be charged a penalty.		

TASK 5   **(Total 7 marks)**

(a)   Calculate the amount of output VAT that should be accounted for on the following supplies for a trader in standard-rated manufactured components.   **(5 marks)**

	Goods pre discount price £	Trade discount	Prompt payment discount	Customer qualifies for prompt payment discount	Output tax £.p
(i)	1,000	10%	None	Not applicable	
(ii)	2,000	Nil	5%	Yes	
(iii)	750	8%	None	Not applicable	
(iv)	1,900	Nil	3%	No	
(v)	3,924	7%	5%	Yes	

(b)   Edgar has completed his VAT return for his latest quarter. It correctly shows VAT due to HMRC of £4.578.95. The last quarter's VAT payment of £6,397.68 has been entered in the VAT account on the wrong side.   **(2 marks)**

What is the **uncorrected** balance showing on the VAT account? Choose ONE answer.

A   £10,976.63 VAT due to HMRC

B   £17,374.31 VAT due to HMRC

C   £1,818.73 due from HMRC

D   £8,396.41 due from HMRC

TASK 6   **(Total 7 marks)**

You have been given the following information about the business transactions of Illusion Ltd for the quarter ended 31 December 20X3.

	£
Sales of standard-rated items	250,000
Purchases of standard-rated goods	162,000
Purchases of zero-rated goods	21,500

You are also told that

1   There is an 8 month old irrecoverable debt on a sales invoice for £1,250 including VAT and a 5 month old irrecoverable debt on a sales invoice for £1,212 excluding VAT. These have both been written off in the accounts.

2   A non-deliberate error was made in the previous return. Output tax was understated by £3,200.12.

3   All figures are VAT-inclusive unless told otherwise.

(a)   Calculate the figure to be claimed for irrecoverable debt relief. £...................................

(b)   Calculate the VAT due on sales and other outputs (Box 1). £...................................

(c)   Calculate the VAT reclaimed in the period on purchases and other inputs (Box 4).

        £...

TASK 7   (Total 17 marks)

The following has been extracted from the company's ledgers for the quarter ended 31 March 20X1:

Sales: UK

Date		£.pp
31/01/20X1	Sales day-book	212,630.00
28/02/20X1	Sales day-book	305,000.00
31/03/20X1	Sales day-book	286,250.00

Sales: Export EU (VAT-registered businesses)

Date		£.pp
31/01/20X1	Sales day-book	25,150.00
28/02/20X1	Sales day-book	14,920.00
31/03/20X1	Sales day-book	19,879.00

Sales: Export non-EU

Date		£.pp
31/01/20X1	Sales day-book	15,600.00
28/02/20X1	Sales day-book	9,820.00
31/03/20X1	Sales day-book	16,780.00

Purchases: UK

Date		£.pp
31/01/20X1	Purchases day-book	68,350.00
28/02/20X1	Purchases day-book	75,213.00
31/03/20X1	Purchases day-book	71,456.00

Output VAT

Date		£.pp
31/01/20X1	Sales day-book	42,526.00
28/02/20X1	Sales day-book	61,000.00
31/03/20X1	Sales day-book	57,250.00

Input VAT

Date		£.pp
31/01/20X1	Purchases day-book	13,670.00
28/02/20X1	Purchases day-book	15,042.60
31/03/20X1	Purchases day-book	14,291.20

Additional information

- VAT returns are completed quarterly.

- Today's date is 18 April 20X1.

- The following items have not been included in the records:

    - acquisitions of goods worth £14,780 from an EU VAT-registered supplier

    - purchases of services of £17,500 from an EU VAT-registered supplier.

Complete Boxes 1 to 9 of the VAT return for the quarter ended 31 March 20X1.

		£
VAT due in the period on **sales** and other outputs	**Box 1**	
VAT due in the period on **acquisitions** from other **EU Member States**	**Box 2**	
Total VAT due (**the sum of boxes 1 and 2**)	**Box 3**	
VAT reclaimed in the period on **purchases** and other inputs, including acquisitions from the EU	**Box 4**	
Net VAT to be paid to HM Revenue & Customs or reclaimed (**Difference between boxes 3 and 4**)	**Box 5**	
Total value of **sales** and all other outputs excluding any VAT. **Include your box 8 figure**	**Box 6**	
Total value of purchases and all other inputs excluding any VAT. **Include your box 9 figure**	**Box 7**	
Total value of all **supplies** of goods and related costs, excluding any VAT, to other **EU Member States**	**Box 8**	
Total value of all **acquisitions** of goods and related costs, excluding any VAT, from other **EU Member States**	**Box 9**	

TASK 8 (Total 10 marks)

(a)   You are an accounting technician. The company financial accountant has asked you to deal with the VAT return for the quarter ended 30 June 20X5. An extract is given below.

		£
VAT due in the period on **sales** and other outputs	**Box 1**	29,562.58
VAT due in the period on **acquisitions** from other **EU Member States**	**Box 2**	1,963.49
Total VAT due (**the sum of boxes 1 and 2**)	**Box 3**	
VAT reclaimed in the period on **purchases** and other inputs, including acquisitions from the EU	**Box 4**	19,868.65
Net VAT to be paid to HM Revenue & Customs or reclaimed (**Difference between boxes 3 and 4**)	**Box 5**	

Complete the following email to the financial accountant advising him of the amount of VAT that will be paid or received and the date due. **(7 marks)**

Today's date is 16 July 20X5.

Email
To:
From:
Date:
Subject: VAT return
Please be advised that I have just completed the VAT return for the quarter ended
(   ).
The amount of VAT **(payable/receivable)** will be £ (   ).
This will be **(paid electronically by   )/(received directly into our bank account)**
Kind regards

(b)   You work for a company that pays its VAT by direct debit.

The accountant asks you when the company's VAT payment for the quarter ended 31 March will be taken from the company bank account.

Today's date is Wednesday 23 April.

Assume bank working days are Monday to Friday only and that there is a Bank Holiday on 12 May. Choose one date from the list below.   **(3 marks)**

A   30 April

B   10 May

C   13 May

D   14 May

Section 4

MOCK ASSESSMENT ANSWERS

TASK 1

(a) (i) 30 April 20X2

The trader exceeds the registration threshold after 10 months trading – by the end of March 20X2. He must notify HMRC by 30 days after exceeding the threshold.

(ii) 1 May 20X2.

(iii) Yes – Any business that makes some taxable supplies can register voluntarily.

(b)

	True	False
A business has an expected turnover for the next 12 months of £87,000 but it sells goods that are zero-rated so it cannot register for VAT.		✓
VAT records should normally be kept for 4 years.		✓
Business records that should be kept include order books.	✓	
If you want to find out information about registering for VAT the first thing you should do is write to HMRC for information.		✓
It is important for an AAT member to keep up to date to ensure client confidentiality.		✓
If a business fails to register for VAT then HMRC will collect any VAT due but will not issue a penalty.		✓

Tutorial note

*Traders who make zero-rated supplies are making taxable supplies and **can** register for VAT.*

Records should be kept for 6 years. Business records that should be kept include:

– *annual accounts, including statements of profit or loss (i.e. income statements)*

– *bank statements and paying-in slips*

– *cash books and other account books*

– *orders and delivery notes*

> – *purchase and sales books*
>
> – *records of daily takings such as till rolls*
>
> – *relevant business correspondence*
>
> *The first place to look for information about VAT is on the HMRC website.*
>
> *Although they are both included in the AAT Code of Professional Ethics, it is important to keep up-to-date to ensure professional competence, not client confidentiality.*
>
> *If a business fails to register for VAT it may be issued with a penalty.*

Key answer tips

Information about this topic is included in the indirect tax reference material provided in the real assessment, so you do not need to learn it.

However you need to be familiar with its location and content – why not look at it now?

TASK 2

(a)   The answer is B

Tutorial note

The basic tax point is the date by which the goods must be accepted provided that is less than 12 months after the date the goods were sent.

However, if the goods are accepted before this date then the date of acceptance becomes the tax point.

(b)   The answer is C

The amount payable will decrease by £8. The VAT on the credit note is £8 (£40 × 20%) and this will reduce the amount the business needs to pay HMRC. This has the same effect as VAT on a purchase.

(c)   The correct answer is C

A partially-exempt business has to apportion input tax in proportion to the levels of taxable and exempt supplies.

However, if the exempt input tax is below the de minimis limit the whole of the input tax can be recovered.

(d)

	Item	Number (1, 2, or 3)
A	Identifying number	1
B	Delivery date	3
C	Total amount of VAT payable	1
D	Customer's registration number	3

Key answer tips

Information about this topic is included in the indirect tax reference material provided in the real assessment, so you do not need to learn it.

However you need to be familiar with its location and content – why not look at it now?

TASK 3

(a)   The answer is C

Tutorial note

The annual accounting scheme is not useful for businesses that are experiencing lower turnover than the previous year as the liability is based on the previous year's turnover not the current year.

For repayment businesses, they would have to wait longer for their refund if they are only completing one return per annum.

(b)   (i)   The answer is £698 (£6,980 × 10%).

The POAs are always based on the previous year's VAT liability.

(ii)   The answer is £929.

The POAs are paid at the end of months 4 to 12 so there are nine instalments.

(9 months × £698) = £6,282 paid during the year.

This year's liability is £7,211 so the difference is the balancing payment

i.e. (£7,211 – £6,282) = £929

(c)

	True	False
Irrecoverable (bad) debt relief is available for all debts written off by a business provided the debt is over 3 months old.		✓
A business has prepared its VAT return for the quarter ended 31 March 20X2; it must pay by electronic transfer by 30 April 20X2.		✓

Tutorial note

Irrecoverable (bad) debt relief is available if the debt is over 6 months old.

Payments are due 1 month and 7 days after the end of the VAT quarter with an extra 3 bank working days if paying by direct debit.

Key answer tips

Information about this topic is included in the indirect tax reference material provided in the real assessment, so you do not need to learn it.

However you need to be familiar with its location and content – why not look at it now?

TASK 4

(a)

Item	Net £	VAT £	Gross £	Reclaim?
Motor car	2,500.00	500.00	3,000.00	✗
Stationery	25.00	5.00	30.00	✓
Fixtures and fittings	1,212.00	242.40	1,454.40	✓
Staff entertaining	250.00	50.00	300.00	✓

(b)

		On next return	Separate disclosure
(i)	A business with a net error of £15,552 and a turnover of £2,800,000.	✓	
(ii)	A business with a net error of £8,032 and a turnover of £58,000.	✓	
(iii)	A business with a net error of £12,156 and a turnover of £810,000.		✓

Tutorial note

When a trader discovers a VAT error they must inform HMRC. If the net error is less than a certain threshold and is not deliberate, it can be included on the next VAT return. If not, it must be disclosed separately on Form VAT 652 or in a letter.

The threshold operates as follows:

Net errors up to £10,000 can always be included on the next VAT return.

Net errors above £50,000 must always be separately disclosed.

Errors between these thresholds can be included on the next VAT return if they are no more than 1% of turnover (specifically the figure in Box 6 of the return).

(c)

	True	False
A business that always pays it's VAT on time, but for the first time submits its VAT return late, will not be issued with a surcharge liability notice.		✓
If a business makes a careless error it must notify HMRC and may be charged a penalty.	✓	

Tutorial note

When a business pays its VAT late or submits its VAT return late, it is in default. The first time that this happens the business will receive a surcharge liability notice. This warns them that if returns or payments are made late in the next 12 months then they may receive a penalty known as a surcharge.

All errors must be notified to HMRC in the approved manner. Careless or deliberate errors may suffer a penalty.

TASK 5

(a) (i) £180.00 (£1,000 × 90% × 20%)

(ii) £380.00 (£2,000 × 95% × 20%)

(iii) £138.00 (£750 × 92% × 20%)

(iv) £380.00 (£1,900 × 20%)

(v) £693.37 (£3,924 × 93% × 95% × 20%)

> *Tutorial note*
>
> For a supply of goods VAT is always calculated on the amount that the customer finally pays.
>
> VAT on an invoice can be rounded down to the nearest penny.

(b)   The answer is B

A VAT payment should be debited to the VAT account but it has been credited in error.

This means that the account is showing too many credits.

The credit side is £12,795.36 (2 × £6,397.68) too high and the uncorrected balance must be £17,374.31 (£4,578.95 + £12,795.36).

TASK 6

(a)   Irrecoverable (bad) debt relief is £208.33 (£1,250 × 20/120)

(b)   VAT due on sales and other outputs £44,866.78 (W1)

(c)   VAT reclaimed on purchases and other inputs £27,208.33 (W2)

Workings:

(W1)   **Box 1**

		£.pp
VAT on standard-rated sales	(£250,000 × 20/120)	41,666.66
VAT error		3,200.12
		44,866.78

(W2)   **Box 4**

	£.pp
VAT on purchases of standard-rated goods (£162,000 × 20/120)	27,000.00
Irrecoverable (bad) debt relief	208.33
	27,208.33

Tutorial note

There has to be at least 6 months since the later of the due date for payment of the invoice or the date of supply before the VAT can be reclaimed. Therefore the VAT on the 5 month old invoice cannot be reclaimed until next quarter.

When a trader discovers a VAT error they must inform HMRC. If the net error is less than a certain threshold and is not deliberate, it can be included on the next VAT return. If not, it must be disclosed separately on Form VAT 652 or in a letter.

The threshold operates as follows:

- *Net errors up to £10,000 can always be included on the next VAT return.*
- *Net errors above £50,000 must always be separately disclosed.*

Errors between these thresholds can be included on the next VAT return if they are no more than 1% of turnover (specifically the figure in Box 6 of the return).

TASK 7

VAT return for the quarter ended 31 March 20X1

		£
VAT due in the period on **sales** and other outputs	**Box 1**	164,276.00
VAT due in the period on **acquisitions** from other **EU Member States**	**Box 2**	2,956.00
Total VAT due **(the sum of boxes 1 and 2)**	**Box 3**	167,232.00
VAT reclaimed in the period on **purchases** and other inputs, including acquisitions from the EU	**Box 4**	49,459.80
Net VAT to be paid to HM Revenue & Customs or reclaimed **(Difference between boxes 3 and 4)**	**Box 5**	117,772.20
Total value of **sales** and all other outputs excluding any VAT. **Include your box 8 figure**	**Box 6**	923,529
Total value of purchases and all other inputs excluding any VAT. **Include your box 9 figure**	**Box 7**	247,299
Total value of all **supplies** of goods and related costs, excluding any VAT, to other **EU Member States**	**Box 8**	59,949
Total value of all **acquisitions** of goods and related costs, excluding any VAT, from other **EU Member States**	**Box 9**	14,780

Workings

		£.pp
Box 1 – Output tax		
31/01/X1		42,526.00
28/02/X1		61,000.00
31/03/X1		57,250.00
VAT on supplies of services from EU supplier	(£17,500 × 20%)	3,500.00
		164,276.00
Box 2 – VAT due on acquisitions	(£14,780 × 20%)	2,956.00
Box 4 – Input tax		
31/01/X1		13,670.00
28/02/X1		15,042.60
31/03/X1		14,291.20
VAT on supplies of services from EU supplier		3,500.00
VAT due on acquisitions		2,956.00
		49,459.80

	£
Box 6 – Total outputs	
UK sales (£212,630 + £305,000 + £286,250)	803,880
EU sales (£25,150 + £14,920 + £19,879)	59,949
Non-EU sales (£15,600 + £9,820 + £16,780)	42,200
Supplies of services from EU supplier	17,500
	923,529
Box 7 – Total inputs	
31/01/X1	68,350
28/02/X1	75,213
31/03/X1	71,456
Supplies of services from EU supplier	17,500
Acquisitions from EU supplier	14,780
	247,299
Box 8 – EU Sales	
31/01/X1	25,150
28/02/X1	14,920
31/03/X1	19,879
	59,949

KAPLAN PUBLISHING

Tutorial note

1   *Export sales are dealt with as follows:*

Sales to registered businesses in the EU are called despatches and are zero-rated so there is no output VAT to include in Box 1. The sales are part of the total outputs included in Box 6 and are also entered in Box 8.

Sales to non VAT-registered customers in the EU are treated just like normal UK sales and are not included in Box 8.

Sales to customers outside the EU are zero-rated and they only appear on the VAT return as part of the outputs in Box 6.

2   *Acquisitions (purchases from EU registered suppliers) – VAT is included in Boxes 2 and 4 and the net amount of the purchase in Boxes 7 and 9.*

3   *Imports of services from EU VAT-registered businesses are dealt with under the 'reverse charge' principle – that is they are treated as if the business supplied the services to itself. The VAT is included in Box 1 and then reclaimed in Box 4. The net amount of the supply is included as a sale in Box 6 and a purchase in Box 7.*

TASK 8

(a)   Email to Financial Accountant

	Email
To:	Financial Accountant
From:	Accounting Technician
Date:	16 July 20X5
Subject:	VAT return

Please be advised that I have just completed the VAT return for the quarter ended **30 June 20X5**.

The amount of VAT **payable** will be **£11,657.42**.

This will be **paid electronically by 7 August 20X5**.

Kind regards

Workings

VAT payable = (£29,562.58 + £1,963.49 – £19,868.65) = £11,657.42

(b)   The answer is C

The normal payment date is 7 days after 30 April i.e. 7 May.

If 23 April is a Wednesday then so is 30 April and 7 May.

Payments by direct debit are taken from the business bank account 3 working days after the normal payment date. Three working days after Wednesday 7 May will be Tuesday May 13. (Saturdays, Sundays and Bank Holidays are not working days so are excluded.)

Key answer tips

Information about this topic is included in the indirect tax reference material provided in the real assessment, so you do not need to learn it.

However you need to be familiar with its location and content – why not look at it now?